UNLOCKING THE BIBLE

OLD TESTAMENT BOOK II

A Land and a Kingdom

UNLOCKING THE BIBLE

OLD TESTAMENT BOOK II

A Land and a Kingdom

David Pawson

with Andy Peck

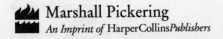

Marshall Pickering
An Imprint of HarperCollins*Publishers*

Marshall Pickering is an imprint of
HarperCollins*Religious*
Part of HarperCollins*Publishers*
77–85 Fulham Palace Road, London W6 8JB

First published in Great Britain in 1999
by HarperCollins*Religious*

1 3 5 7 9 10 8 6 4 2

A catalogue record for this book is
available from the British Library

ISBN 0 551 03188 3

Printed and bound in Great Britain by
Caledonian International Book Manufacturing Ltd, Glasgow

CONTENTS

INTRODUCTION

I suppose this all started in Arabia, in 1957. I was then a chaplain in the Royal Air Force, looking after the spiritual welfare of all those who were not C.E. (Church of England) or R.C. (Roman Catholic) but O.D. (other denominations – Methodist to Salvationist, Buddhist to atheist). I was responsible for a string of stations from the Red Sea to the Persian Gulf. In most there was not even a congregation to call a 'church', never mind a building.

In civilian life I had been a Methodist minister working anywhere from the Shetland Islands to the Thames Valley. In that denomination it was only necessary to prepare a few sermons each quarter, which were hawked around a 'circuit' of chapels. Mine had mostly been of the 'text' type (talking about a single verse) or the 'topic' type (talking about a single subject with many verses from all over the Bible). In both I was as guilty as any of taking texts out of context before I realized that chapter and verse numbers were neither inspired nor intended by God and had done immense damage to Scripture, not least by changing the meaning of 'text' from a whole book to a single sentence. The Bible had become a compendium of 'proof-texts', picked out at will and used to support almost anything a preacher wanted to say.

With a pocketful of sermons based on this questionable technique, I found myself in uniform, facing very different congregations – all male instead of the lifeboat-style gatherings I had been used to: women and children first. My meagre stock of messages soon ran out. Some of them had gone down like a lead balloon, especially in compulsory parade services in England before I was posted overseas.

So here I was in Aden, virtually starting a church from scratch, from the Permanent Staff and temporary National Servicemen of Her Majesty's youngest armed service. How could I get these men interested in the Christian faith and then committed to it?

Something (I would now say: Someone) prompted me to announce that I would give a series of talks over a few months, which would take us right through the Bible ('from Generation to Revolution'!).

It was to prove a voyage of discovery for all of us. The Bible became a new book when seen as a whole. To use a well-worn cliché, we had failed to see the wood for the trees. Now God's plan and purpose were unfolding in a fresh way. The men were getting something big enough to sink their teeth into. The thought of being part of a cosmic rescue was a powerful motivation. The Bible story was seen as both real and relevant.

Of course, my 'overview' was at that time quite simple, even naive. I felt like that American tourist who 'did' the British Museum in 20 minutes – and could have done it in 10 if he'd had his running shoes! We raced through the centuries, giving some books of the Bible little more than a passing glance.

But the results surpassed my expectations and set the course for the rest of my life and ministry. I had become a 'Bible teacher', albeit in embryo. My ambition to share the excitement of knowing the whole Bible became a passion.

When I returned to 'normal' church life, I resolved to take my congregation through the whole Bible in a decade (if they put up with me that long). This involved tackling about one 'chapter' at every service. This took a lot of time, both in preparation (an hour in the study for every 10 minutes in the pulpit) and delivery (45–50 minutes). The ratio was similar to that of cooking and eating a meal.

The effect of this systematic 'exposition' of Scripture confirmed its rightness. A real hunger for God's Word was revealed. People began to *come* from far and wide, 'to recharge their batteries' as some explained. Soon this traffic was reversed. Tape recordings, first prepared for the sick and housebound, now began to *go* far and wide, ultimately in hundreds of thousands to 120 countries. No one was more surprised than I.

Leaving Gold Hill in Buckinghamshire for Guildford in Surrey, I found myself sharing in the design and building of the Millmead Centre, which contained an ideal auditorium for continuing this teaching ministry. When it was opened, we decided to associate it with the whole Bible by reading it aloud right through without stopping. It took us 84 hours, from Sunday evening until Thursday morning, each person reading for 15 minutes before passing the Bible on to someone else. We used the 'Living' version, the easiest both to read and to listen to, with the heart as well as the mind.

We did not know what to expect, but the event seemed to capture the public imagination. Even the mayor wanted to take part and by sheer coincidence (or providence) found himself reading about a husband who was 'well known, for he sits in the council chamber with the other civic leaders'. He insisted on taking a copy home for his wife. Another lady dropped in on her way to see her solicitor about the legal termination of her marriage and found herself reading, 'I hate divorce, says the Lord.' She never went to the lawyer.

An aggregate of 2,000 people attended and bought half a ton of Bibles. Some came for half an hour and were still there hours later, muttering to themselves, 'Well, maybe just one more book and then I really must go.'

It was the first time many, including our most regular attenders, had ever heard a book of the Bible read straight through. In most churches only a few sentences are read each week and then not always consecutively. What other book would get anyone interested, much less excited, if treated in this way?

So on Sundays we worked through the whole Bible book by book. For the Bible is not one book, but many – in fact, it is a whole library (the word *biblia* in Latin and Greek is plural: 'books'). And not just many books, but many *kinds* of books – history, law, letters, songs, etc. It became necessary, when we had finished studying one book, and were starting on another, to begin with a special introduction covering very basic questions: What kind of book is this? When was it written? Who wrote it? Who was it written for? Above all, *why* was it written? The answer to that one provided the 'key' to unlock its message. Nothing in that book could be fully understood unless seen as part of the whole. The context of every 'text' was not just the paragraph or the section but fundamentally the whole book itself.

By now, I was becoming more widely known as a Bible teacher and was invited to colleges, conferences and conventions – at first in this country, but increasingly overseas, where tapes had opened doors and prepared the way. I enjoy meeting new people and seeing new places, but the novelty of sitting in a jumbo jet wears off in 10 minutes!

Everywhere I went I found the same eager desire to know God's Word. I praised God for the invention of recording cassettes which, unlike video systems, are standardized the world over. They were helping to plug a real hole in so many places. There is so much successful evangelism but so little teaching ministry to stabilize, develop and mature converts.

I might have continued along these lines until the end of my active ministry, but the Lord had another surprise for me, which was the last link in the chain that led to the publication of these volumes.

In the early 1990s, Bernard Thompson, a friend pastoring a church in Wallingford, near Oxford, asked me to speak at a short series of united meetings with the aim of increasing interest in and knowledge of the Bible – an objective guaranteed to hook me!

I said I would come once a month and speak for three hours about one book in the Bible (with a coffee break in the middle!). In return, I asked those attending to read that book right through before and after my visit. During the following weeks preachers were to base their sermons and house group discussions on the same book. All this would hopefully mean familiarity at least with that one book.

My purpose was two-fold. On the one hand, to get people so interested in that book that they could hardly wait to read it. On the other hand, to give them enough insight and information so that when they did read it they would be excited by their ability to understand it. To help with both, I used pictures, charts, maps and models.

This approach really caught on. After just four months I was pressed to book dates for the next five years, to cover all 66 books! I laughingly declined, saying I might be in heaven long before then (in fact, I have rarely booked anything more than six months ahead, not wanting to mortgage the future, or presume that I have one). But the Lord had other plans and enabled me to complete the marathon.

Anchor Recordings (72, The Street, Kennington, Ashford, Kent TN24 9HS) have distributed my tapes for the last 20 years and when the Director, Jim Harris, heard the recordings of these meetings, he urged me to consider putting them on video. He arranged cameras and crew to come to High Leigh Conference Centre, its main hall 'converted' into a studio, for three days at a time, enabling 18 programmes to be made with an invited audience. It took another five years to complete this project, which was distributed under the title 'Unlocking the Bible'.

Now these videos are travelling around the world. They are being used in house groups, churches, colleges, the armed forces, gypsy camps, prisons and on cable television networks. During an extended visit to Malaysia, they were being snapped up at a rate of a thousand a week. They have infiltrated all six continents, including Antarctica!

More than one have called this my 'legacy to the church'. Certainly it is the fruit of many years' work. And I am now in my seventieth year on planet earth, though I do not think the Lord has finished with me yet. But I did think this particular task had reached its conclusion. I was mistaken.

HarperCollins approached me with a view to publishing this material in a series of volumes. For the last decade or so I had been writing books for other publishers, so was already convinced that this was a good means of spreading God's Word. Nevertheless, I had two huge reservations about this proposal which made me very hesitant. One was due to the way the material had been prepared and the other related to the way it had been delivered. I shall explain them in reverse order.

First, I have never written out in full any sermon, lecture or talk. I speak from notes, sometimes pages of them. I have been concerned about communication as much as content and intuitively knew that a full manuscript interrupts the rapport between speaker and audience, not least by diverting his eyes from the listeners. Speech that is more spontaneous can respond to reactions as well as express more emotions.

The result is that my speaking and writing styles are very different, each adapted to its own function. I enjoy listening to my tapes and can be deeply moved by myself. I am enthusiastic about reading one of my new publications, often telling my wife, 'This really *is* good stuff!' But when I read a transcript of what I have said, I am ashamed and even appalled. Such repetition of words and phrases! Such rambling, even incomplete sentences! Such a mixture of verb tenses, particularly past and present! Do I really abuse the Queen's English like this? The evidence is irrefutable.

I made it clear that I could not possibly contemplate writing out all this material in full. It has taken most of one lifetime anyway and I do not have another. True, transcripts of the talks had already been made, with a view to translating and dubbing the videos into other languages such as Spanish and Chinese. But the thought of these being printed as they were horrified me. Perhaps this is a final struggle with pride, but the contrast with my written books, over which I took such time and trouble, was more than I could bear.

I was assured that copy editors correct most grammatical blunders. But the main remedy proposed was to employ a 'ghostwriter' who was in tune with me and my ministry, to adapt the material for printing. An introduction to the person chosen, Andy Peck, gave me every confidence that he could do the job, even though the result would not be what I would have written – nor, for that matter, what he would have written himself.

I gave him all the notes, tapes, videos and transcripts, but these volumes are as much his work as mine. He has worked incredibly hard and I am deeply grateful to him for enabling me to reach many more with the truth that sets people free. If one gets a prophet's reward for merely giving the prophet a drink of water, I can only thank the Lord for the reward Andy will get for this immense labour of love.

Second, I have never kept careful records of my sources. This is partly because the Lord blessed me with a reasonably good memory for such things as quotations and illustrations and perhaps also because I have never used secretarial assistance.

Books have played a major role in my work – three tons of them, according to the last furniture remover we employed, filling two rooms and a garden shed. They are in three categories: those I have read, those I intend to read and those I will never read! They have been such a blessing to me and such a bane to my wife.

The largest section by far is filled with Bible commentaries. When preparing a Bible study, I have looked up all relevant writers, but only after I have prepared as much as I can on my own. Then I have both added to and corrected my efforts in the light of scholarly and devotional writings.

It would be impossible to name all those to whom I have been indebted. Like many others I devoured William Barclay's *Daily Bible Readings* as soon as they were issued back in the 1950s. His knowledge of New Testament background and vocabulary was invaluable and his simple and clear style a model to follow, though I later came to question his 'liberal' interpretations. John Stott, Merill Tenney, Gordon Fee and William Hendrickson were among those who opened up the New Testament for me, while Alec Motyer, G. T. Wenham and Derek Kidner did the same for the Old. And time would fail to tell of Denney, Lightfoot, Nygren, Robinson, Adam Smith, Howard, Ellison, Mullen, Ladd, Atkinson, Green, Beasley-Murray, Snaith, Marshall, Morris, Pink and many many others. Nor must I forget two remarkable little books from the pens of women: *What the Bible is all about* by Henrietta Mears and *Christ in all the Scriptures* by A. M. Hodgkin. To have sat at their feet has been an inestimable privilege. I have always

regarded a willingness to learn as one of the fundamental qual-
ifications to be a teacher.

I soaked up all these sources like a sponge. I remembered
so much of *what* I read, but could not easily recall *where* I had
read it. This did not seem to matter too much when gathering
material for preaching, since most of these writers were pre-
cisely aiming to help preachers and did not expect to be constantly quoted. Indeed, a sermon full of attributed quotations
can be distracting, if not misinterpreted as name-dropping
or indirectly claiming to be well read. As could my previous
paragraph!

But printing, unlike preaching, is subject to copyright,
since royalties are involved. And the fear of breaching this held
me back from allowing any of my spoken ministry to be repro-
duced in print. It would be out of the question to trace back 40
years' scrounging and even if that were possible, the necessary
footnotes and acknowledgements could double the size and
price of these volumes.

The alternative was to deny access to this material for
those who could most benefit from it, which my publisher per-
suaded me would be wrong. At least I was responsible for col-
lecting and collating it all, but I dare to believe that there is
sufficient original contribution to justify its release.

I can only offer an apology and my gratitude to all those
whose studies I have plundered over the years, whether in
small or large amounts, hoping they might see this as an example of that imitation which is the sincerest form of flattery. To
use another quotation I read somewhere: 'Certain authors,
speaking of their works, say 'my book' ... They would do better
to say 'our book' ... because there is in them usually more of
other people's than their own' (the original came from Pascal).

So here is 'our' book! I suppose I am what the French
bluntly call a 'vulgarizer'. That is someone who takes what the

academics teach and makes it simple enough for the 'common' people to understand. I am content with that. As one old lady said to me, after I had expounded a quite profound passage of Scripture, 'You broke it up small enough for us to take it in.' I have, in fact, always aimed to so teach that a 12-year-old boy could understand and remember my message.

Some readers will be disappointed, even frustrated, with the paucity of text references, especially if they want to check me out! But their absence is intentional. God gave us his Word in books, but not in chapters and verses. That was the work of two bishops, French and Irish, centuries later. It became easier to find a 'text' and to ignore context. How many Christians who quote John 3:16 can recite verses 15 and 17? Many no longer 'search the scriptures'; they simply look them up (given the numbers). So I have followed the apostles' habit of naming the authors only – 'as Isaiah or David or Samuel said'. For example, the Bible says that God whistles. Where on earth does it say that? In the book of Isaiah. Whereabouts? Go and find out for yourself. Then you'll also find out when he did and why he did. And you'll have the satisfaction of having discovered all that by yourself.

One final word. Behind my hope that these introductions to the Bible books will help you to get to know and love them more than you did lies a much greater and deeper longing – that you will also come to know better and love more the subject of all the books, the Lord himself. I was deeply touched by the remark of someone who had watched all the videos within a matter of days: 'I know so much more about the Bible now, but the biggest thing was that I felt the heart of God as never before.'

What more could a Bible teacher ask? May you experience the same as you read these pages and join me in saying: Praise Father, Son and Holy Spirit.

J. David Pawson
Sherborne St John, 1999

Yes, I thought I knew my Bible,
Reading piecemeal, hit or miss:
Now a part of John or Matthew,
Then a bit of Genesis.

Certain chapters of Isaiah,
Certain psalms, the twenty-third,
First of Proverbs, twelfth of Romans –
Yes, I thought I knew the Word.

But I found that thorough reading
Was a different thing to do
And the way was unfamiliar
When I read my Bible through.

You who like to play at Bible,
Dip and dabble here and there,
Just before you kneel all weary,
Yawning through a hurried prayer.

You who treat this crown of writings
As you treat no other book:
Just a paragraph disjointed,
Just a crude impatient look.

Try a worthier procedure,
Try a broad and steady view;
You will kneel in awesome wonder
When you read the Bible through.

Author unknown

OVERVIEW OF THE OLD TESTAMENT

God has given us a library of 66 books. The Latin word *biblia*, translated as 'bible', literally means 'books'. The 39 Old Testament books, which cover over 2,000 years, are written by a variety of authors and include many types of literature. It is no surprise, therefore, that many people come to the Bible wondering how it all fits together.

God did not arrange the Bible topically so that we could study themes individually: he arranged it so that we could read a book at a time. The Bible is God's truth about himself and how we should relate to him, set in the context of history. It tells how people, principally the nation of Israel, came to experience God for themselves and respond to his Word. Far from being a dry theological textbook, it is the vibrant story of God's redeeming work in the lives of his people.

Many fail to grasp the overall message because they have an insufficient understanding of the background to the Bible. This chapter aims to provide an overview of the Old Testament so that any particular portion of Scripture can be given its correct context.

Geography

If we are to understand the Old Testament there are two maps we need to appreciate first of all: those of the Promised Land and the Middle East.

The key area in the map of the Middle East is what geographers call 'the Fertile Crescent' – the band of fertile land which stretches from the River Nile in Egypt in the west, north-east through the land of Israel and then south and south-east to the plains surrounding the rivers Tigris and Euphrates in what used to be called Mesopotamia (which means 'the middle of the rivers', *meso* – 'middle' and *potamia* – 'rivers'). This fertile area comprised the centres of power in the ancient world, with Egypt located in the west and Assyria and later Babylon in the east. Israel was wedged between these two and much of the Old Testament is written with the struggles between these world powers in the background. There are also significant times when their threats or activities impinge directly on Israel.

Israel's geographical position made it significant as a trade route. The Syrian Desert to the east of Israel meant that traders and armies from the orient needed to cross Israel's border as they moved between Asia, Africa and Europe. A mountainous area of basalt rock to the south-west of the Sea of Galilee funnelled the travellers through Jezreel and on through to Megiddo. A great trunk road entered Palestine through the Syrian Gate, running through Damascus, across the Bridge of Jacob's Daughters and over a basalt dam to the Lake of Galilee. It then ran south-west via the Plains of Megiddo to the Coast Plain, through Lydda and Gaza to Egypt. Israel was a narrow corridor – to the east was the rift valley, which ran north to south down to the Dead Sea, and to the west was the Mediterranean Sea.

Israel, therefore, was at the crossroads of the world, with trade routes arriving from all directions and Megiddo the place

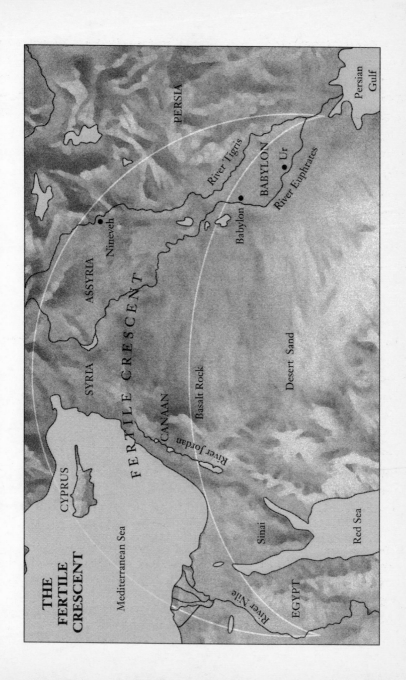

THE
FERTILE
CRESCENT

Mediterranean Sea

CYPRUS

FERTILE CRESCENT

CANAAN

SYRIA

ASSYRIA

Nineveh

River Jordan

Basalt Rock

Sinai

EGYPT

River Nile

Red Sea

PERSIA

River Tigris

BABYLON

Ur

River Euphrates

Babylon

Desert Sand

Persian Gulf

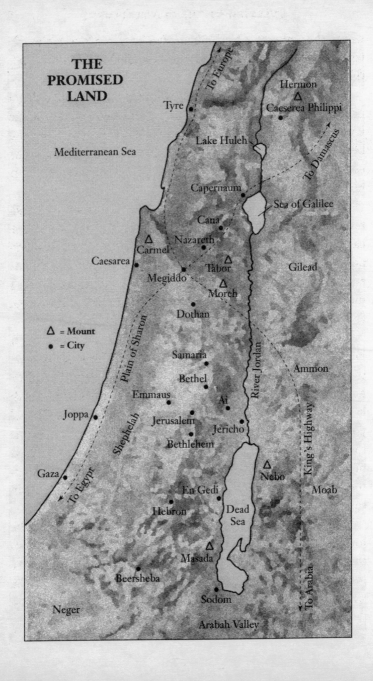

THE
PROMISED
LAND

Mediterranean Sea

To Europe

Tyre

Hermon
Caeserea Philippi

Lake Huleh

To Damascus

Capernaum

Sea of Galilee

Cana

Nazareth

Carmel

Caesarea

Tabor

Megiddo

Gilead

Moreh

Dothan

△ = Mount
• = City

Plain of Sharon

Samaria

Bethel

River Jordan

Ammon

Emmaus

Ai

Joppa

Shephelah

Jerusalem

Jericho

Bethlehem

King's Highway

Nebo

Gaza

To Egypt

En Gedi

Moab

Hebron

Dead
Sea

Masada

To Arabia

Beersheba

Sodom

Neger

Arabah Valley

where they all met. Overlooking this 'crossroads' was the village of Nazareth, and doubtless Jesus would have sat on the hill there and watched the world go by.

This location has spiritual significance. God was planting a people at a crossroads where they could be a model of the kingdom of heaven on earth. The whole world could see the blessing that comes to people living under God's rule – and the curse that comes when they disobey. Israel's unique position is no accident.

Turning to the internal geography of the Promised Land, the northern part containing the crossroads of the world was called Galilee, or 'Galilee of the Nations' because of its international flavour. The southern part, Judaea, was more mountainous and isolated from the rest of the world, encouraging a more distinctively Jewish culture with the capital of Jerusalem at its centre.

The Promised Land is about the same size as Wales, but it includes every kind of climate and scenery. Wherever you live, there is somewhere in Israel that is just like home. The place most like England is just south of Tel Aviv. Carmel in the north is known as 'Little Switzerland'. Just 10 minutes from Carmel you can sit down among palm trees. Prominent in the land is the River Jordan, which rises on Mount Hermon and runs north to south within the rift valley mentioned earlier, through the Sea of Galilee and down to the Dead Sea. A fertile plain surrounds its course.

All the flora and fauna of Europe, Africa and Asia can be found in Israel. Scots pine trees grow next to palm trees from the Sahara. In biblical times the wild animals in the country included lions, bears, crocodiles and camels. It seems as if the whole world was somehow squeezed into one small country.

History

Having made ourselves familiar with the general geography of the Old Testament world, we now need to consider an outline of the history of the Old Testament. It may sound daunting to have to cover 2,000 years or more, but a simple chart will help us to grasp the basics (see p. 7).

The Old Testament covers over 2,000 years of history before the time of Christ. Genesis 1–11 covers the 'prehistoric' part – the creation of the universe, the Fall of man in the Garden of Eden, the Flood and the Tower of Babel. The focus here is on humankind in general, though including a 'godly' line. But we can chart the history of Israel itself from 2000 BC, when God calls Abraham (though it would be centuries before the nation was formed).

The Old Testament period can be divided into four equal parts of roughly 500 years each. Each period has a key event, a prominent person and a type of leadership.

2000	1500	1000	500
Election	Exodus	Empire	Exile
Abraham	Moses	David	Isaiah
Patriarchs	Prophets	Princes	Priests

In the first period the patriarchs led Israel: Abraham, Isaac, Jacob and Joseph. In the second period Israel was led by prophets, from Moses to Samuel. In the third period they were led by princes (kings), from Saul to Zedekiah. The fourth period saw the priests take the lead, from Joshua (a priest who returned to Judah from exile under Zerubbabel's rule) to Caiaphas in the time of Christ.

None of the leader types was ideal and each individual brought his own flaws to the task. The nation needed a leader

BIRTH, DEATH, RESURRECTION, ASCENSION [JESUS]
MATTHEW, MARK, LUKE, JOHN

(O.T.) HEBREW HISTORY (BC)

2000	1500	1000	500
Election	Exodus	Empire	Exile
Abraham	Moses	David	Isaiah
PATRIARCHS	**PROPHETS**	**PRINCES**	**PRIESTS**
(Abraham to Joseph)	*(Moses to Samuel)*	*(Saul to Zedekiah)*	*(Joshua to Caiaphas)*

ABRAHAM
ISAAC
JACOB

400 YEAR GAP — GOD SILENT INACTIVE

JOSEPH

GENESIS 12–50

JOB?

EGYPT
INDIA
CHINA

EXODUS
LEVITICUS
NUMBERS
DEUTERONOMY

JOSHUA
JUDGES
RUTH

SAUL
DAVID
SOLOMON

'ISRAEL' (10)
'JUDAH' (2)
ELIJAH
ELISHA

1, 2 SAMUEL
1, 2 KINGS
1, 2 CHRONICLES

PSALMS
S of S.
PROV.
ECCL.

BEFORE
JOEL   JONAH
AMOS   NAHUM
HOSEA   OBADIAH
MICAH   HABAKKUK
ISAIAH   ZEPHANIAH

DURING
JEREMIAH
(LAMENTATIONS)
EZEKIEL

AFTER
HAGGAI
ZECHARIAH
MALACHI

DANIEL
ESTHER

EZRA
NEHEMIAH

400 YEAR GAP — GOD SILENT INACTIVE

SOCRATES
PLATO
ARISTOTLE

BUDDHA
CONFUCIUS
ALEXANDER THE GREAT
JULIUS CAESAR

CREATION, FALL, FLOOD, BABEL [MAN]
GENESIS 1–11

who was prophet, priest *and* king, and they found him in Jesus. Each stage, therefore, was a foreshadowing of the ideal leader who was to come.

This time line is broken by two 400-year gaps. The first comes between the patriarchs and the prophets around 1500 BC and the second after the priests at 400 BC. During these two sets of 400 years God said nothing and did nothing, so there is nothing in the Bible from those two periods. There were some Jewish books written in the second of these two periods, known collectively as the Apocrypha, but they are not part of the Bible proper because they do not cover the time when God was speaking and acting. Malachi is therefore the last book in the Old Testament of our standard English Bibles, then there is a 400-year gap before Matthew's Gospel.

It is especially interesting to note the events in world history which took place during these two gaps. The Egyptian, Indian and Chinese cultures developed during the first gap, while in the second Greek philosophy developed through Socrates, Plato and Aristotle. Other great figures of this time include Buddha, Confucius, Alexander the Great and Julius Caesar. So much happened which historians regard as important, but it was of little relevance to God. It was *his* history with *his* people which really mattered.

A brief overview of the books

Genesis 12–50 covers the first period of Israel's history when the nation was led by the patriarchs (see the table given above). It is possible that the book of Job was written at this time, since there are parallels with the sort of life the patriarchs would have lived.

Relatively few books cover the next quarter. Exodus, Leviticus, Numbers and Deuteronomy were all written by

Moses. The books of Joshua, Judges and Ruth continue the history of that period.

There are more books associated with the third quarter: Samuel, Kings and Chronicles, plus the poetic books: Psalms, Proverbs, Ecclesiastes and Song of Solomon. During this third quarter and after Solomon's time there was a civil war when the 12 tribes divided into two parts, the 10 tribes in the north calling themselves Israel, the two in the south Judah. This is the end of the united nation. There were prophets during that time – Elijah and Elisha – but they were 'non-book' prophets.

Finally there are a large number of prophetic books associated with the Exile (the northern kingdom of Israel fell to the Assyrians, then the tribes in the southern kingdom of Judah were forced into exile by the Babylonians). Some contain prophecies from before the Exile, some during it, some after, and some have a mixture because the prophet overlaps more than one phase. This tells us something of the importance of this event to Israel's history. It meant the loss of the land God had promised them and struck at the heart of their identity as a nation.

Prophets warned the people that they were going to lose the land and prophets (sometimes the same ones) comforted them when they did lose the land. There were prophets urging them to rebuild the temple when they returned to Judah after 70 years away. The books of Daniel and Esther are written from Babylon itself. The prophets Ezra and Nehemiah helped to rebuild Jerusalem and renew the people once they had returned.

This brief outline is enough to demonstrate that the books of the Old Testament are not always in chronological order. The 'history books' are fairly accurately arranged, but the prophets are organized according to size not chronology. Hence it can be confusing to know who was speaking when.

The rise and fall of a nation

There is another aspect of the chart given on page 7 which is worth underlining. The chart shows a dotted line representing the fortunes of the nation, which reach their height under David and Solomon. The line's gentle rise indicates the progress up to this point, with a sharp drop once the peak is reached. Every Jew looks back to that period and longs for it to return. It was the golden age. They look for a son of David to restore their prosperity.

The last question the disciples asked Jesus before he ascended to heaven was about when he would restore the kingdom to Israel. They are asking the same question 2,000 years later.

The line continues its descent until Israel is exiled by Assyria in 721 BC and then Judah by Babylon in 587 BC.

Following the 400-year gap John the Baptist arrives, the first prophet for a long time. Then comes the life and ministry of Jesus. The New Testament covers 100 years compared to the 2,000-plus years of the Old Testament.

The order of the books

We have noted already that the chronology of Old Testament history is different from the order in which the books appear. There is also a big difference in the order of books as included in the English Old Testament compared with the Hebrew Bible. The English Bible is arranged in terms of **history**: Genesis to Esther, then **poetry**: Job to Song of Solomon, then **prophecy**: Isaiah to Malachi. The prophets are further split into the **major prophets**: Isaiah, Jeremiah, Ezekiel and Daniel, and the **minor prophets**: Hosea to Malachi. However, the descriptions 'major' and 'minor' are given because of the size of the book and nothing else. These divisions are generally highlighted in the contents page, if at all, so most readers are unaware of the change of category when they move from one section to the next.

The Hebrew Scriptures have three clear divisions. The first five books are not regarded as history but as **law**, and are known by the first words read as the scroll was unrolled. The next section goes under the title of **prophets**, a surprising title because it includes a number of books listed in the English Bible as history. Joshua, Judges, Samuel and Kings are called the **former prophets**, with the major and minor prophets (as they are called in the English Bible) listed as **latter prophets**. This is because the Jews see the history books as prophetic history – history according to how *God* perceived what was happening and what was important. All history is based on the principle of selection and connection – what is included and why it is included. The Bible's history is no exception, except that it is the prophets under God's inspiration who make the selection.

Ruth and the books of Chronicles are history within the English Bible but are not regarded as prophetic history within the Hebrew Bible. Indeed, there is no direct action of God mentioned in the book of Ruth, although the people in the story refer to him for blessings, and so on. Instead these books form part of the **writings**, the third and last division in the Hebrew Scriptures. There are more surprises here, for the poetry books are included, and Daniel, who we might expect to be included among the prophetic books.

This division may seem odd, but it is the division that Jesus refers to when he appears to the two on the road to Emmaus and the ten disciples, following his death and resurrection. We read about how he took them through the law, the prophets and the writings, and showed them everything concerning himself. This was the Old Testament division Jesus knew and accepted and I believe we could find it helpful too.

There are other Jewish history books which are not part of the Bible. The books of the Apocrypha are mostly 'history', although some contain other types of literature. They include fascinating stories, offering insights into the life of the Maccabees in their rebellion against the Greeks who occupied the land in the centuries before Christ. But these books were not judged to be records inspired by God and so were not included when the Old Testament canon was finally agreed. They have been incorporated into Roman Catholic Bibles.

The law: the foundation of the Old Testament

If we are to grasp fully the message of the Old Testament and of the whole Bible, it is vital that we read and understand the first five books, Genesis to Deuteronomy, known variously as the Law, the Torah, or the Pentateuch. They are foundational for all that follows. They explain how the nation of Israel started and developed, and why the people behaved as they did. They are the basis of the prophetic messages towards the end of the Old Testament, as the prophets urge the people to return to their covenant obligations outlined in the law.

The books of the law create an interesting pattern (see also Old Testament Volume 1, 'The Maker's Instructions', of this series).

- Genesis is concerned with the whole human race.
- Exodus is the beginning of Israel's national life.
- Leviticus is concerned with one tribe, the Levites.

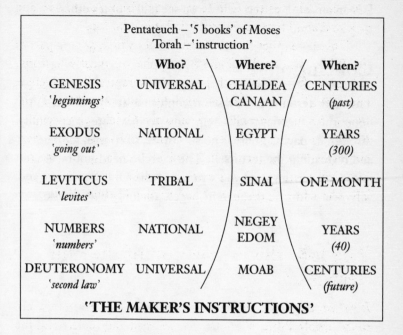

Pentateuch – '5 books' of Moses
Torah – 'instruction'

	Who?	Where?	When?
GENESIS *'beginnings'*	UNIVERSAL	CHALDEA CANAAN	CENTURIES *(past)*
EXODUS *'going out'*	NATIONAL	EGYPT	YEARS *(300)*
LEVITICUS *'levites'*	TRIBAL	SINAI	ONE MONTH
NUMBERS *'numbers'*	NATIONAL	NEGEY EDOM	YEARS *(40)*
DEUTERONOMY *'second law'*	UNIVERSAL	MOAB	CENTURIES *(future)*

'THE MAKER'S INSTRUCTIONS'

Then note how the focus expands again:

- Numbers is concerned with national life (as in Exodus).
- Deuteronomy looks again to the history of the whole world (as in Genesis).

Furthermore, we can see a similar pattern with the time each book covers:

- Genesis covers centuries.
- Exodus covers 300 years.
- Leviticus covers just one month.
- Numbers covers 40 long years (Israel wandering in the desert).
- Deuteronomy covers centuries again (looking ahead to Israel's future).

It is an amazing pattern when you see it all put together.

Conclusion

The Old Testament may seem confusing at first sight, but I hope this overview will help you to navigate successfully through its pages. There is no substitute, of course, for reading and re-reading the text itself. The exercise need not be academic. God has inspired the writing of the Old Testament and will meet with you through its pages. You only have to ask.

PART I

JOSHUA

Introduction

A schoolteacher asked a classroom of children who knocked down the walls of Jericho. There was a long silence before a small boy said, 'Please sir, I didn't!'

Later that day in the staffroom, the teacher recounted the incident to the headmaster. 'Do you know what happened in my classroom today? I asked who knocked down the walls of Jericho and that boy Smith said, "Please sir, I didn't."'

The headmaster replied, 'Well, I've known Smith some years and I know his family – they're a good family. If he says he didn't do it, I'm sure he didn't.'

The headmaster later reported the boy's answer to a visiting school inspector, whose response was: 'It's probably too late to find out who did it; get them repaired and send the bill to us.'

The joke, of course, is that everybody should know who knocked down the walls of Jericho. It is one of the better known stories in the Bible. If they do not know the story from the Bible, then they have heard the Negro spiritual song 'Joshua fit the battle of Jericho'. But this is the only part of the book many people do know. Joshua is not a well known book and a knowledge of the battle does not mean that everyone believes it actually happened. For even this story raises questions: How were the walls knocked down? Were they, in fact, knocked down at all?

It is clear that there are a number of preliminary questions for us to consider as we look at the book of Joshua. First of all we need to ask what sort of a book it is and how we should read the incredible stories it contains. We will then go on to look at the content and structure of the book, and how Christians can read it for maximum benefit.

What kind of a book is Joshua?

Joshua is the sixth book in the Old Testament. In our English Bible it is the book after Deuteronomy, with an apparently logical flow from the death of Moses at the end of Deuteronomy to the commissioning of Moses' successor Joshua at the start of the next book. To the Jews, however, the significance of the book's position is quite different. The end of Deuteronomy marks the end of the Torah, the law of Moses. These five books are read annually in the synagogue, with Genesis 1:1 beginning the New Year and the end of Deuteronomy being read at its end. Each of the five books is named after its first words, since these would be the words seen at the start of the scroll when the books came to be selected for reading. Joshua is the first book to be known by the name of its author.

Joshua is also a completely new type of literature. The first five books of the Bible set out the basic constitution of the people of Israel and are foundational to all that follows. By contrast, there is not a single law in Joshua, or in the books that follow. In Joshua we begin to see how the law is worked out in practice.

Joshua tends to be regarded as a history book because it comes in what is regarded as the history section of the English Bible. But it is more than just a history book. As we saw in the Overview of the Old Testament (pages 1–14), the Jews divide the Old Testament into three sections, rather like a library with books collected under three categories. The first five are the 'books of the law', also called the Torah or the Pentateuch. The 'books of the prophets' come next. Joshua is the first book of the 'former prophets', followed by Judges, 1 and 2 Samuel, and 1 and 2 Kings. The books of Isaiah to Malachi comprise the 'latter prophets', with a few exceptions. The third section is 'the writings', which includes Psalms, Job, Proverbs, Ruth, Song of Songs, Ecclesiastes, Lamentations, Esther, Daniel, Ezra, Nehemiah, and 1 and 2 Chronicles. So two books which are in the English Bible as prophets – Daniel and Lamentations – are part of 'the writings' in the Jewish Old Testament arrangement. Chronicles is the last book of the writings, although the English Bible includes it in the history section.

Joshua's inclusion as a book of prophecy under the Jewish arrangement surprises many, for most of it is in narrative form and reads more like straight history than the poetic prophecy of later books. There are, however, a number of reasons why we should concur with this 'prophecy' tag.

First, it is not widely known that Joshua was a prophet. It is true that he is better known as a military commander, but he was a prophet just like Moses in that he heard from God and spoke for God. Indeed, the last chapter of the book records Joshua, in the first person singular, delivering God's message to the people.

Second, biblical history is in any case a special kind of history. There are two principles which have to be followed when writing any history:

■ **Selection** – it is impossible to include everything, even when covering a short period of time. The Bible's history is highly selective, focusing largely on one nation and only on certain events within that nation's life.
■ **Connection** – a good historian takes seemingly disparate events and shows how they link together, so that a common theme is developed.

Using these two principles, we can see why the history in Joshua and the other 'history' books in the Bible is in fact *prophetic*. The author selects the events which are significant to God or are explained by God's activity. Only a prophet can write this kind of history, for only a prophet has insight into what to include and why. Seeing the book as prophecy reminds us that the real hero of the book is not Joshua but God (and this applies to any book of the Bible). We see God's activity in this world, what he says and what he does. Therefore, whilst it is genuine history, in that it describes what happened, we must see it as *prophetic* history, for it declares the reality of God and his work in the world.

The chart below shows the contrast between the books of the 'former prophets' and the books of the law.

FIRST FIVE BOOKS	NEXT SIX BOOKS
Genesis	Joshua
Exodus	Judges
Leviticus	1 and 2 Samuel
Numbers	1 and 2 Kings
Deuteronomy	
LAW (TORAH)	PROPHETS (FORMER)
PROMISE	FULFILMENT
GRACE	GRATITUDE
REDEMPTION	RIGHTEOUSNESS
LEGISLATION	APPLICATION
BLESSINGS	OBEDIENCE (LAND GIVEN)
CURSES	DISOBEDIENCE (LAND TAKEN)
COVENENT ESTABLISHED	COVENANT EXPRESSED
CAUSE	EFFECT

There are a number of things to note from this chart.

1 The law includes **God's promises to Israel**. The former prophets describe **how these promises were fulfilled**.

2 The law is **God's grace** expressed to the people. The former prophets show **how the people responded in gratitude** to what they heard (although, as we will see, this gratitude was often sadly lacking).

3 The books of the law describe **God's redemption of his people** from Egypt (Exodus). The former prophets explain **how the people were to respond** to God's initiative by living in righteousness.

4 The books of the law tell how **God would bless obedience and punish disobedience**. In Joshua we see **how an obedient response led to victory**, as in the battle of Jericho. Conversely, we also see the ramifications of disobedience to the law, as in the defeat at Ai. Continued disobedience meant that the land claimed in the book of Joshua was taken away in 2 Kings.

The former prophets tell the tragic story of how the people won the Promised Land through obedience to the law, but then forfeited it because of disobedience. To put it another way: the first five books are the cause and the next six books the effect.

How should we read Joshua?

Before focusing on the book of Joshua itself we need to deal with the scholarly debate which can undermine our reading of so much biblical history. Many scholars argue that biblical truth is not historical or scientific but moral and religious. They are quite happy to accept that miraculous events form part of the Bible – just as long as no one is expected to believe that they actually took place! They suggest that biblical history is 'myth' or 'legend', teaching spiritual truths or values but not describing actual events which took place.

We need not deny that parts of the Bible are fictional. Jesus' parables are technically 'myths'. It does not matter whether there was an actual prodigal son or not, since the purpose of the story was to communicate important truth to the hearers. However, admitting that the Bible contains stories is a long way from agreeing that events included in the Bible are fiction.

Questioning the truth of the Bible began in the nineteenth century, when scholars argued that Adam and Eve were not real people but mythological figures whose activities explain universal truths. They said that the Fall was not the entrance of sin into the world, with a real Adam and Eve eating fruit prohibited by God, but a story showing the universal truth that if you tell someone not to touch something, they will want to touch it!

This approach did not stop with the story of Adam and Eve. Noah's ark was next and eventually there were few biblical events which escaped this type of scrutiny. After this we were apparently left with a kind of biblical version of *Aesop's Fables*, which conveys spiritual truth but has minimal historical basis.

The process of reading the Bible from this standpoint was given a long name: *demythologization*. Put simply, this means that in order to obtain the truth, one must discard the story (myth), and with it any suggestion that the story is based on historical fact. Miraculous or supernatural elements can therefore be discarded as being part of the myth.

This demythologization did not stop with the Old Testament: the New Testament was also attacked. The virgin birth, the miracles and the resurrection were regarded as soft targets. This scholarly debate affected theological training, and before long there were church leaders who taught that it did not matter whether the resurrection actually took place, providing people *believed* that it did. They said that if Jesus' bones did still lie rotting in Israel, it made no difference to our 'faith'.

With this background in mind, it is no surprise to find that concerns have been raised regarding elements of the book of Joshua, not least the story of the fall of Jericho. Scholars reasoned that the miracles in the story could not be accepted as fact by readers in a sophisticated scientific age. They saw it instead merely as a tale teaching us that God wants us to win our battles.

However, demythologizing Joshua requires much of the book to be cut out, for there are many apparent myths within the book: the Jordan river dries up, the Jericho walls collapse, hailstones help win a battle, and the sun and moon stand still for a whole day.

How do we respond to such an attempt to undermine the historical value of Joshua?

1 If we were to accept that miracles do not happen, we would be left with a purely human history, with little or no spiritual benefit. **God's part would be totally excluded**. The 'values' or 'truths' would be of no more value than the sort of lessons gleaned, for example, from the secular history of China.

2 Mythical writings invent places and people to distinguish the genre from proper history, but biblical history is completely different. **Joshua includes real places** we can visit today: the River Jordan, Jericho and Jerusalem. **It also includes real people groups**, which secular historians acknowledge existed at this time: the Canaanites and the Israelites.

3 Joshua claims to be **written by contemporary eyewitnesses**. The first person plural 'we' is used, for the writers were reflecting on events they had seen. Furthermore, a common phrase in the text is 'to this day'. Contemporaries of the writer could check out the details. This is not a fable about mythical characters, but a sequence of historical events described by people who were there.

4 **Archaeologists confirm a great deal of information given in Joshua**. They have discovered that the entire culture of some of the cities included in the book changed over a 50-year period. There is evidence that cities such as Hazor, Bethel and Lachish were destroyed between 1250 and 1200 BC and the inhabitants reverted to a far simpler lifestyle. The date of this change fits with Joshua's account of how these cities were conquered.

5 Those who question the miraculous events in Joshua ignore the fact that the events in themselves are not necessarily miraculous. It is no problem for us to accept the miraculous, but it is interesting to note that such phenomena can be explained. For example, the River Jordan dries up during floods even today. The river meanders through the Jordan Valley and, because of the flood conditions, undercuts the banks on the curve. These banks can be so undercut that they collapse, causing the river to dam itself, sometimes for up to five hours. Similarly, in modern times, we know that large buildings collapse. Cathedrals and skyscrapers have fallen in the same manner as the walls described in Joshua. **It is not the events that are miraculous so much as the *timing***. The river dries up and the walls fall just when God said they would.

6 We have noted already that the Bible is not the history of Israel as such, for there is much that is excluded. Joshua covers 40 years, yet most of what happened in those 40 years is not recorded. The fall of Jericho fills about three chapters, which is out of all proportion if this is a history of Israel. **It is really the history of what the God of Israel did**. The writer records the periods when God was at work, for he is a living God, active in time and history, saying and doing things. If God had not intervened on their behalf, the Israelites would never have got the Promised Land. It was

an impossible task for a bunch of ex-slaves with no military training to go in and take a well-fortified land and replace a culture that was far superior to theirs in humanistic terms. If the subject of the book is God's activity, therefore, it should be no surprise when his work is beyond human understanding. If we seek to remove these parts of the story, or to 'demythologize' them, we undermine the whole nature and purpose of the book.

Questions about whether the Bible is myth or history boil down to a personal question: Do we believe in a *living* God? If our answer is yes, then we can go on to look at the Bible as a record of what he said and did and ask why he said and did these things.

The Bible is not just about God, or even just about the God of Israel. It is the history of God *and* Israel – the story of their relationship – and that is how we need to read every book of the Old Testament, including Joshua. It is not fanciful to see God's relationship with Israel as a marriage. The engagement took place with Abraham when God promised to be the God of Abraham and his descendants. The wedding took place at Sinai when the people heard the obligations and promises tied up with the law and agreed to play their part in the binding agreement God was introducing. The honeymoon was supposed to last for three months, as the people journeyed to the Promised Land. The bride, however, was not ready or willing to trust her husband, so it was 40 years before they finally entered the land. In Joshua we have the beginning of their life together in a prepared place, their new home. They were given the title deeds but still had to enter the land and take it. Sadly the marriage did not work out and there was even a temporary divorce, the faults being on the 'wife's side'. Since God hates divorce, however, he never left them.

The content of Joshua

It is important that we gain an overview of the content of Joshua before looking at the detail. This will save us from drawing inappropriate or unwarranted conclusions about what it means, just as we would refuse to judge a novel by selecting isolated pages without seeing the whole thing. Every sentence in a book takes its meaning from the context, so we need to see the book as a whole first.

The book covers the life of Joshua from the age of 80 to 120. This 40-year period matches exactly the length of Moses' leadership, also between the ages of 80 and 120, which is covered by Exodus, Leviticus, Numbers and Deuteronomy. The difference between the two is that Moses was a lawgiver and a leader while Joshua was just a leader, the period of lawgiving having been completed.

Structure

The book divides like a sandwich. There are three parts: two thin slices of bread and a lot of filling in the middle.

- The top 'slice' is **Chapter 1**, the prologue describing **Joshua's commissioning** as leader.
- The bottom 'slice' is **Chapters 23 and 24**, Joshua's **final sermon** and his **death and burial**.

The main section between these two outer 'slices' is the account of how Israel possessed the land that God had promised them, in spite of the fact that it was already occupied. This middle section can be further divided:

- **Chapters 2–5** cover the **entering** of the land of Canaan through the River Jordan.

- **Chapters 6–12** detail how they **conquered** the land, with a list of the 24 kings that Joshua defeated being given in Chapter 12.
- **Chapters 13–22** cover the **dividing** of the land between the tribes who had conquered it.

Joshua's commission

Joshua was 80 years of age when he received his call to serve as a leader. It is possible to identify two parts to the call: divine encouragement and human enthusiasm.

DIVINE ENCOURAGEMENT

God tells Joshua that he is his choice to replace Moses following his death. Moses had led Israel out of Egypt, and now Joshua would lead them into the Promised Land. God promises that just as he had been with Moses, so he would be with Joshua. He tells him to be strong, courageous and careful to obey the law. If he does this he will prosper.

It is an encouraging, if challenging, beginning to his leadership. The word 'prosperous' has been misunderstood. It does not mean 'wealthy', and those claiming that the Bible promises financial rewards are mistaken. It means that Joshua will achieve what he sets out to achieve in God's name.

These words of encouragement were not merely for Joshua's wellbeing. God knew that his leadership would affect the morale of the whole people of Israel. And important as it was that Joshua's leadership should help morale, he was also to ensure that his own morality was of the highest standard. He was not just leading a group of individuals armed for battle who needed good pep talks, he was leading the people of God. Their standards of morality would affect their success in battle too, and Joshua was to set an example.

HUMAN ENTHUSIASM

When Joshua told the people of God's decision they were enthusiastic – indeed, their precise response echoes the commands God had given him privately, for they also urge Joshua to 'be strong and courageous'. Furthermore, they promise to obey him fully just as they had obeyed Moses. This may seem strange, as the Israelites' behaviour under Moses' leadership could hardly be described as obedient and this was one of the reasons why they had taken 40 years to travel to the Promised Land. But this new generation had learned from the disobedience of their forefathers. This generation had obeyed Moses whilst he had been alive, when they had conquered Moab and Ammon, and were now comfortable about reaffirming their support for the new man. They promise specifically to do what Joshua tells them and to go where he sends them. They ask that God may be with Joshua as he was with Moses.

This twofold aspect of Joshua's calling is instructive for calls to service today. Both aspects are required: a God-given sense that an individual is called to the work, and a heartfelt response from God's people that this is so.

Joshua's command

The heart of the book deals with Joshua leading the people as they enter the land of Canaan. There are three sections, all dealing fundamentally with the land.

1. ENTERING

(i) Before

Before entering, Joshua sends two spies into the land. When 12 spies had been sent out 40 years before, the negative report from 10 of them had contributed to Israel's faithless refusal to enter the land. This time just two are asked to go in, mirroring the number who had brought back a good report on that first occasion. Sending in spies may seem to be faithless – after all, had God not promised the land to them? But they were practising a principle Jesus used in a story when he was on earth: it is important to sit down and count the cost before you go to battle. It would have been foolhardy for the Israelites to enter Canaan without first obtaining the maximum amount of information about what they might face.

The place where the spies stayed tells us a lot about the moral state of Canaan. They ended up staying in a brothel with a prostitute named Rahab. It is clear from their conversation with Rahab that news of the Israelite victories over Egypt and the surrounding nations had made the locals fearful about their prospect of repelling an invasion. Indeed, Rahab was so convinced that God would give the land to Israel that she wanted to join them. The New Testament commends this amazing display of faith, for Rahab is included in the great heroes of the faith mentioned in Hebrews.

The means of her escape was reminiscent of the way in which the Jewish first-born escaped with their lives when the angel of death came to Egypt. They had painted blood from the Passover lamb on the door frames of their houses. Rahab was told to hang a scarlet thread out of the window so that she and her family would be spared the destruction that would come on the city of Jericho. It was as if she was marking her window with blood, so that death would not touch her home. Not only was she commended for her faith, but Matthew's Gospel records how this prostitute is included in the royal lineage which reaches to Jesus himself. It is an extraordinary and moving tale.

(ii) During
The River Jordan operated like a moat on the eastern edge of Canaan, especially at harvest times when floods could reach

depths of 20 feet, with no bridges or fords to enable easy cross-
ings. We have noted already that it is likely that a temporary
natural dam upstream stopped the flow of the river to enable
the people to cross. The timing was perfect: the river bed was
dry at the precise moment when the priest at the front of the
convoy entered the river.

The miracle enabled the crossing but also had an
additional purpose. Many of the new generation of people who
entered the land with Joshua had not witnessed the miracle of
the crossing of the Red Sea recorded in the book of Exodus.
God wanted his people to see his mighty power and to have
confidence in the leadership of Joshua as he led them against
the Canaanites and into the Promised Land. God was with him
as he had been with Moses.

(iii) After
Their first camp in the Promised Land was at Gilgal, an open
space near to the fortified town of Jericho which had been built
to guard the eastern approach up to the hills. When the
Israelites arrived they did three things:

1 They **took 12 stones from the bed of the River Jordan
  and made a cairn** as a reminder for future generations of
  how God had dried up the river. Remembrance was an
  important part of Old Testament piety. Israel had as part of
  their culture many reminders of what God had done for
  them in the past. A cairn of stones was a favourite method
  of marking a significant site, with the 12 stones representing the 12 tribes.
2 They **circumcised all the men**. The new generation had
  not undergone this covenant rite, first introduced with
  Abraham. Joshua wanted to follow the law to the letter –
  the people's spiritual condition was important.

3 They **named the place Gilgal, which means 'rolled'**, because God had 'rolled away' the reproach or disgrace of Egypt.

God also did something when they entered the land: he stopped sending manna. For 40 years the Israelites had fed off this daily provision, but now they had reached the fertile land of Canaan, 'a land flowing with milk and honey', and the manna was redundant. Even today there are delicious grapefruits and oranges sold in Jericho.

(iv) The captain of the Lord's host
Jericho was the first city they were to attack, but before the battle Joshua had an unusual experience. He approached the city by night to see the fortifications for himself and was met by an armed man.

Joshua suspected this man was an enemy and asked whether he was friend or foe. He was surprised to receive the answer 'No', a nonsensical reply! But then the man added that he was not part of the Hebrew or Canaanite peoples, but belonged to God's forces, involved with heavenly rather than earthly troops. He was virtually asking Joshua whose side *he* was on! The person was none other than the captain of the Lord's host, i.e. a senior angel, an archangel or even the pre-incarnate Son of God himself. Joshua was being reminded that he was not the highest officer in the Lord's army, but only an under-officer. The experience also made clear to him that he did not fight alone, nor was he the true commander of Israel – he was a servant of God and the people.

2. CONQUERING
The military strategy for taking the land is clear – they were to divide and conquer. Joshua drove a wedge straight through the

middle of Canaan and then, having divided the enemy into two halves, he conquered the south then the north. This strategy prevented the forces in Canaan from uniting, and meant that Israel could fight manageable numbers, dealing with each area in turn.

The view that Joshua is prophetic history is underlined by the space given to the first two cities attacked. Jericho and Ai were deemed the most significant. The moral lessons, both positive success and negative failure, learned from these two inital assualts, would be confirmed in later engagements; but the prophetic interpretation would not need to be repeated.

(i) The centre
Jericho
Ancient Jericho is a mile down the road from modern Jericho. Its ruins today are at Tel Es Sultan and reveal that Jericho is the oldest city in the world, dating from 8000 BC and containing the oldest building in the world, a round tower with a spiral staircase inside. These remains have been excavated and, of course, the key question was whether the walls which fell in Joshua's day could be found. In the 1920s the archaeologist John Garstang thought he had found them, only to be contradicted by Kathleen Kenyon, who asserted that Jericho was not even occupied in Joshua's day! However, the Egyptologist David Rohl has revised the dating and discovered fallen walls and burned buildings at another level in the diggings (see his remarkable book *The Test of Time*, Century, 1995, following the TV series of the same name, which includes his discovery of remains of Joseph's time in Egypt, and his even more remarkable *Legend: The Genesis of Civilisation*, Century, 1998, locating the Garden of Eden, still full of fruit trees - and he's not even a believer!)

When Jericho eventually fell, Joshua cursed anyone who sought to rebuild it. He said that their first-born would die when the foundations were laid, and their youngest would die when the gates were put in place. The book of Kings records an attempt to rebuild the city 500 years later, when the curse was enacted exactly as predicted. Although one would expect building work to take place on the ruins, therefore, the curse was a real deterrent. The remains of Jericho were left open to the weather and available to anyone wishing to remove stonework for other buildings. The absence of some walls thus helps to confirm the truth of the Bible's record.

Archaeologists have confirmed the size of the walls from similar constructions. They suggest that Jericho's walls were 30 feet high, with a 6-foot thick outer wall and a 12–15-foot gap between that and a 12-foot thick inner wall. The walls became a barrier as the city grew, so houses were perched on the top of the walls in close proximity to one another. It is easy to see how an earth tremor could send the whole lot toppling down. The text tells us that the sustained noise of the horns of 40,000 men was the trigger, so maybe this sound was sufficient – rather in the way that an opera singer can crack a light bulb if she sings at a certain intensity and pitch. The only house that remained standing was the one with the scarlet thread hanging from the window – the house of the prostitute Rahab, preserved because of her faith in the God of Israel.

The destruction was so great that no fighting was necessary – the Israelites simply walked in and took the city. But victory celebrations were conditional. God told them that this city was his, rather like the 'first fruits' of the harvest. They must recognize that this was God's victory, not theirs. The cities conquered in the future could be looted, but not Jericho. One man, however, disobeyed the command, and this fact links with the next story.

Ai

The flourishing city of Ai was farther up the hill from Jericho. But this time the battle was lost. Israel made two errors. The first was over-confidence: Joshua used fewer troops, believing that conquering this city would be as easy as it had been with Jericho. They learnt the important lesson that it is fatal to think that because God has blessed you once, he is going to do it again in the same way.

The man who took some of the loot from Jericho made the second error. Achan had taken a Babylonian robe, 200 shekels of silver and a wedge of gold weighing 50 shekels, thinking that these items' disappearance would not be noticed. When Joshua's troops first attacked Ai, they were routed and they fled. Joshua was distraught and asked God why he had let this happen, especially now that their reputation was growing. God explained that Israel had sinned; one of them had taken something devoted to God. So they drew lots to find the tribe, then the clan, then eventually Achan's family.

Lots may seem a strange way of deciding on an issue of this magnitude, but the Israelites believed that God was in control of every situation and would enable the person to be identified through the drawing of lots, and so it proved. A similar method was used throughout Israel's history. The priest carried a black stone and a white stone inside his breastplate, called the Urim and Thummim. People would use these to discern what they should do. When the white stone was drawn the answer was positive, and when the black one was drawn it was negative. This practice was continued among God's people right up until the coming of the Holy Spirit at Pentecost. From that moment the Holy Spirit guided his people instead and such methods were never used again.

Achan knew he was guilty. Had he owned up earlier, he might have been forgiven, but he had refused to come clean.

His family were also implicated in the crime because they had
not exposed him, and so they were all stoned to death. It is
frightening that one person's sin could cause a whole people to
suffer such disgrace.

When the sin was dealt with, the Israelites fought against
Ai again and this time they were victorious.

Mount Ebal

Following the destruction of Ai, Joshua led the people of Israel
to two mountains in the centre of the land. Moses had given
clear instructions concerning the renewal of the covenant God
had made with them at Sinai. They were to write the laws he
had given them on uncut plastered stones and then they were
to divide into two groups, one standing on Mount Gerizim
shouting the blessings of the covenant and the other on Mount
Ebal shouting the curses. The two hills form a natural
amphitheatre, so that each group could hear the other and
respond with an 'amen' to what was being called out.

(ii) The south

Despite this covenant affirmation, the people were still fallible,
and they immediately made a big error in their dealings with
the Gibeonites. The Gibeonites were a tribal group within the
land of Canaan who realized that they were unlikely to be able
to stand against an Israelite onslaught. They opted for decep-
tion instead. They visited Israel dressed in old clothes and
shoes and carrying old wineskins, worn-out sacks and stale,
mouldy bread. They claimed to be from a distant country and
said they had heard of Israel and wanted protection.

The text says that the men of Israel took them at face value
and did not enquire of God. Only later did they realize their
error, but by then it was too late, and the four cities belonging
to the Gibeonites had to remain untouched because of the oath

the Israelites had taken to preserve their lives. The Gibeonites were protected by the treaty they had gained through trickery, and served as woodcutters and servants to the people of Israel. Thus Israel was unable to expel these people from the land.

Gibeon continued to be part of the picture. The King of Jerusalem, Adoni-Zedek, heard of the treaty that the Gibeonites had made with Israel and called on four Amorite kings to unite with him and attack Gibeon. The Gibeonites requested Israel's assistance and battle commenced. God assured the Israelites of victory, sending hailstones of such size that more died from the storm than by the sword. It was at this point that Joshua asked for an extraordinary miracle. He knew that he would not be able to continue routing the enemy when it was dark – at sunset all fighting stopped, whatever the state of the battle, since it was impossible to discern who was friend and who was foe. Joshua therefore made an unprecedented prayer request that the sun should stop in order that the battle could continue! This astonishing display of faith was rewarded, and we read that for a full day the sun stopped in the sky. Victory was complete.

I mentioned earlier that such stories have led to doubts about whether the events of Joshua actually happened. It does sound like a fable, doesn't it? Mr Harold Hill, the President of the Curtis Engine Company of the United States, was a consultant to the American Space Program. He wrote the following article in the *Evening World* newspaper in Spencer, Indiana, which later appeared in the *English Churchman* on 15 January 1971:

> I think one of the most amazing things that God has for us today happened recently to our astronauts and space scientists at Green Belt, Indiana. They were checking the position of the sun, moon and planets out in space where they would

be in 100 years and 1,000 years from now. We have to know this in order that we do not send up a satellite and it collides with something later on, on one of its orbits. We have to lay out the orbit in terms of the life of the satellite and where the planets will be so that the whole thing will not go wrong.

They ran the computer measurements backwards and forwards over the centuries and it came to a halt. The computer stopped and put up a red signal which meant that there was something wrong either with the information fed into it or with the results as compared with the standards. They called in the service department to check it out and they said, 'It's perfect.' The head of the operation said, 'What's wrong?'

'Well, we've found there's a day missing in space in a lapsed time.' They were puzzled and there seemed no answer. Then one man on the team remembered he'd been told at Sunday school of the sun standing still. They didn't believe him but as no alternative was forthcoming they asked him to get a Bible and find it – which he did in the book of Joshua 10:12-14 'And the sun stood still, and the moon stayed – and hasted not to go down about a whole day.' The space men said, 'There is the missing day.'

Well, they checked the computers going back into the time it was written and found it was close but not close enough. The elapsed time that was missing back in Joshua's day was 23 hours and 20 minutes – not a whole day. They read the Bible again and it said *about* a day! These little words in the Bible are important. But they were still in trouble because if you can't account for 40 minutes you will be in trouble 100 years from now. Forty minutes had to be found because it can be multiplied many times over in orbits. Then it was this same man who remembered somewhere in the Bible it said the sun went backwards. The space men told him he was out of his mind but they got out the Bible and found how Hezekiah on his death bed was visited by the prophet Isaiah who told him he was not going to die and Hezekiah asked what the sign should be. And Isaiah said 'This sign shalt thou have of the Lord, that the Lord will do the thing that he has spoken: shall the shadow go forward 10 degrees or go back 10 degrees?' And Hezekiah answered 'It is a light thing for the shadow to go down 10 degrees: nay, but let the shadow return backward 10 degrees'. And Isaiah cried unto the Lord: and he brought the shadow 10 degrees backward by which it had gone down in the dial of Ahaz. (2 Kings 20)

Ten degrees is exactly 40 minutes. So 23 hours and 20 minutes in Joshua plus 40 minutes in 2 Kings make the missing 24 hours which they had to log in the log book as being the missing day in the universe.

Those who disbelieve the Bible will no doubt have difficulty accepting this explanation!

The southern campaign continued with victories over Bethel and Lachish (which we know from archaeology were destroyed between 1250 and 1200 BC). The whole region was subdued.

(iii) The north

Having defeated the south, the people turned to concerns in the north. The northern kings were aware of the Israelites' success by then, and so united their forces for battle. Once again, however, God assured the Israelites of victory: their enemies' chariots were burned and their horses hamstrung.

The cities on the mounds were the only ones not totally destroyed, apart from Hazor which Joshua burned. Archaeologists confirm that that city was ruined by fire at this time, between 1250 and 1200 BC.

With the conquests over, we are given an interesting

summary of the Israelites' activity, including the statement that the Lord hardened the hearts of the nations so that they came against Israel in battle. Clearly their sins were so great that complete extermination was the only solution.

3. DIVIDING

Before progressing any further, we must establish the distinction between *occupation* and *subjugation*. Occupation refers to places; subjugation refers to peoples. Whilst the land was theirs, since the people were subjugated, the Israelites still had much land to occupy. Much of the rest of the book is taken up with this process.

The allocation of land was decided by national lottery, leading some to believe that God sanctions the sort of lottery which currently operates in many countries, including Britain. There is, however, an important distinction to be understood. Lotteries are arranged so that humans cannot influence the outcome. Israel chose the lottery specifically so that *God* could influence the outcome. After all, if God could control the sun, this was nothing to him.

(i) The east bank

The land itself is fascinating, and Joshua records how it was surveyed. The same size as Wales, it is the only green part of the Middle East. The Arabian desert lies to the east, the Negev desert to the south. The rain comes from the Mediterranean.

Moses had promised that the Reubenites, the Gadites and the half-tribe of Manasseh would be given fertile land east of the Jordan, providing they helped in the battle for Canaan. Joshua honoured this pledge.

Throughout the division of the land, the key word was 'inheritance'. The land was an inheritance for Israel, not just for a while, nor just for the lifetime of the victors, but as a permanent home to pass on to their descendants.

(ii) The west bank
At Gilgal: 2½ tribes
Caleb was one of the spies who had given a positive report about the land when the 12 spies were sent in 45 years before. Now, at the age of 85, we read that he was just as strong as he had been at 40. He approached Joshua and asked that he might be allowed to take the hill country that he had been promised all those years before. Joshua blessed him and gave him the town of Hebron.

The daughters of Manasseh reminded Joshua of Moses' promise to give them land too. The people of Joseph claimed to be too numerous for the land they were given and so were also allotted forested areas to clear.

The book outlines in considerable detail the towns and villages that were allotted to each tribe, with occasional reference to other matters. We read, for example, of the Israelites' failure to defeat the enemy when Judah could not dislodge the Jebusites in Jerusalem.

At Shiloh: 8½ tribes
Several tribes remained without allotted land, so each tribe selected men to survey the territory in order to divide it further.

(iii) Special cities
Refuge
There were six special cities of refuge, three on each side of the Jordan, where those guilty of manslaughter could flee when they were chased by those intent on revenge. Within Jewish law there was a distinction between accidental, unintentional killing and premeditated killing. These cities enabled the law to be applied.

Levites

When the land had been allotted, the text makes it clear that the Levites received no land as such, no specific territory. We are told that the Lord was their inheritance – serving God was sufficient for them. Of course, the individual Levites had to live somewhere and towns with pastureland were allotted to them, scattered amongst the other tribes.

(iv) The altar on the east bank

Towards the end of Joshua we are told how a potential tragedy was averted. When the two and a half tribes returned across the Jordan to their territories on the east bank, Joshua urged them to be careful to love God, walk in his ways and obey his commands. However, no sooner had they arrived home than they built an altar at Peor, by the Jordan. The other tribes regarded this as idolatry and immediately declared war. Fortunately, they decided to talk before the first blow was struck. The 'guilty' tribes claimed that the new altar was their way of remembering that they were still part of God's people on the other side of the river. This pacified the concerned tribal leaders and war was avoided.

Joshua's commitment

The last two chapters are a moving finale to the book. Joshua was conscious of his advancing years – at 120 he was the same age as Moses was when he died, and had served, like Moses, for 40 years. He knew he was going to die soon and so wanted to make provision for the future of the nation.

It is important to note that whilst Moses appointed Joshua as his successor, Joshua did not appoint a successor for himself. This may seem strange, but from then on the job of leadership could not be left to just one man. The leadership needs were different, the people were scattered across the land, and one man could not lead properly with so much ground to cover. So Joshua passed on his commission to them all.

Joshua's message was very firm: God had promised not only to bless them when they obeyed but to curse them when they disobeyed. God had brought them into the land as he had promised, but they must obey the law if they were to experience his continued favour.

Joshua gave all the credit for Israel's possession of the land to God. Although he had led the people, he recognized that God had fought for them and they should be grateful to him for their success. He concluded his speech by asking the Israelites to take an oath of loyalty to God.

The final chapter is in an altogether different style. Here Joshua speaks in the first person singular as he does in the previous chapter, but this time 'I' means God. His last message is prophecy and is understood as such by the people.

(i) Grace

First God reminds the people of all he has done for them. There is no mention of Joshua's role.

(ii) Gratitude

Now Joshua speaks, urging the people to fear God, serve him, be faithful and throw away any other gods. Then he speaks for himself and his household, saying, 'We will serve the Lord.'

The people agree to follow God with Joshua, who sets up a stone of witness. Three times the people declare, 'We will serve the Lord.'

The last verses of the book record three burials: the burial of Joshua, the burial of Joseph's bones and the burial of Eleazer. For 40 years they had carried with them a coffin containing Joseph's bones, because his dying wish was to be buried in the Promised Land. Now at last the bones could be laid to rest in the land Joseph had looked for.

So a triple funeral rounds off this book. We are told that as long as Joshua and his generation of leaders lived, the people were faithful to God. When the next generation grew up, however, things went badly wrong.

It is possible to sum up the lessons of the book of Joshua in two simple phrases:

- Without God they **could** not have done it.
- Without them God **would** not have done it.

These are two very important lessons. It is easy to put all the responsibility on God or to put it all on ourselves. The Bible has a balance: without God we cannot do it, but without us he will not do it. The change of verb is significant – it is not that without us he cannot, it is that without us he *will* not. If Joshua and the people of Israel had not co-operated with God, their entry into the Promised Land would not have happened, and yet without God and without his intervention, they could not possibly have done it.

Divine intervention

1. GOD'S WORDS

God's words are prominent in the book of Joshua as we hear of his solemn covenant to Israel which he could never break. He had sworn by himself that he would stay with them, and the land was his promised gift. God always keeps his Word – he cannot lie. So Joshua tells us that God gave to Israel all the land he had sworn to their forefathers that he would give them.

2. GOD'S DEEDS

God's deeds are linked with his words. We are told that God would fight for Israel. He would drive the other nations out of the land.

Joshua is full of physical miracles: the division of the River Jordan, the sudden cessation in the provision of manna, the collapse of the Jericho walls, the hailstones which help defeat the five kings, the lengthening of the day by making the sun 'stand still', and the drawing of lots to decide how the land is to be divided.

The book of Joshua is careful to give the glory to God for these amazing events. God was truly with Israel. The name *Immanuel* has four possible meanings or emphases:

1 *God* is with us!
2 God *is* with us!
3 God is *with* us!
4 God is with *us*!

The fourth version conveys the meaning of the biblical text. *Immanuel* means God is on *our* side – the emphasis is that he is going to fight for us, not them. Joshua is a testimony to this truth.

Human co-operation – positive

God works through human co-operation. He did not fight by himself: the Israelites had to go to the battlefield and face the enemy for themselves. Without them God would not have done it – they had to go into the land, they had to take action. God said that every bit of land they actually stood on he would give to them.

1. THEIR ATTITUDE

Not fear (negative)

In taking action and entering the land, the Israelites were not to be afraid. This was the command given to Joshua at the very beginning. This had been the cause of the people's failure 40 years before when they had refused to enter Canaan.

But faith (positive)

If they were to win every battle, their attitude had to be one of confidence and obedience. This faith showed itself in action as they obeyed the Lord's command to march around Jericho seven times in silence, when they doubtless would have preferred to get on and fight straight away. They also had to be prepared to take risks. Joshua took the risk of asking God publicly to stop the sun.

2. THEIR ACTION

Their confidence had to lead to obedience. They were to act on God's Word – they were to do what he said. This is a reminder to us that God's gifts have to be received. The Israelites were given every bit of land they put their foot on, but this meant they had to do something to make the inheritance theirs; it was not automatic.

There is a delicate balance to be reached between faith and action, summed up brilliantly by Oliver Cromwell, who once told his troops, 'Trust in God and keep your powder dry.' Or as C. H. Spurgeon said, 'Pray as if it all depends on God and work as if it all depends on you.'

If the Israelites' attitude was to become self-confident and their action was to become disobedient, however, they would lose every battle. That is why the two major parts of Joshua cover the story of Jericho and the story of Ai, one attack a success, one (initially) a failure. If we learn the lessons of those two towns then we are set for the conquest of the land.

Human co-operation – negative

The Bible is a very honest book. It deals with weaknesses as well as strengths. The book of Joshua tells us about three mistakes the Israelites made when they took over the land.

The first mistake was at Ai. They were defeated by superior troops because they had too much self-confidence. The previous generation had been under-confident, and thus guilty of fear, but this generation was over-confident and therefore guilty of folly. Both attitudes were equally damaging.

The second mistake was when the Gibeonites tricked them into making a treaty to protect them. Their refusal to first ask the Lord what to do is given as the reason for their folly on this occasion.

The third mistake was when the two and a half tribes put up an altar on the east bank of the Jordan and the tribes on the other side of the river accused them of treachery and turning away from the Lord. The misunderstanding that arose almost led to civil war.

Christian application

We are told in 1 Corinthians 10 and Romans 15 that everything in the past was written for our learning. How is the book of Joshua used in the New Testament, and how can we apply what we learn from it today?

Faith

In Hebrews 11 Joshua and Rahab the prostitute are used as examples of faith. They are part of the 'cloud of witnesses' with which we are surrounded.

James says that faith without action is dead; it cannot save us. Again Rahab is used as an example, for the way she hid the spies and said goodbye to the past in order to embrace the faith of Israel.

Sin

The book also gives us a graphic reminder of the problems which sin can cause amongst a whole people. In the New Testament an incident with Ananias and Sapphira exactly matches the sin of Achan. Acts tells the story of how this couple lie about money withheld from the church's common purse, while Achan deceives the people by not owning up to the goods he stole from Jericho. The result in both cases is the same – the judgement of God. Ananias and Sapphira are immediately struck down dead, as Achan was stoned to death by the people.

Salvation

The book is also a glorious picture of salvation. Joshua's name was originally Hoshea, which means 'salvation', but Moses changed it to Yeshua, which means 'God saves'. The Greek version of the Old Testament translates this as 'Jesus'.

Moses himself means 'drawn out', so his name and Joshua's together describe Israel's progress towards the Promised Land. Moses brought them out of Egypt, but it was Joshua the saviour who brought them into the Promised Land. Getting out of Egypt did not constitute salvation, but getting into Canaan did.

This illustrates an important truth: Christians are not just saved *from* something, they are also saved *to* something. It is all too possible to get out of Egypt but still be in the wilderness; to stop living the lifestyle of a nonbeliever but not enjoy the glory of the Christian life.

Applying the concept

Finally we must ask: How should a Christian apply the concept of the Promised Land?

HEAVEN

Some imagine that the Promised Land depicts 'heaven'. One hymn, for example, contains the line: 'When I tread the verge of Jordan, bid my anxious fears subside', as if the image of the river is depicting death, with Canaan (heaven) on the other side.

HOLINESS

The Promised Land, however, is not heaven but holiness.

The writer of Hebrews, commenting on Joshua's conquering of the land, says that the Israelites never entered 'the rest' under Joshua, despite entering Canaan. He goes on to say that there still remains 'a rest' for the people of God. This 'rest' means rest from battle – and the Promised Land is reached when we enjoy what God has for us. So whenever we overcome temptation we have a little foretaste of the rest that God has promised. The victories in Joshua should be replicated in the life of every believer as he or she lives for Christ and battles against sin.

PART II

JUDGES AND RUTH

Introduction

Judges and Ruth belong to each other, so we will consider them together. The Bible is unique among sacred writings in being mostly history. The Koran, for example, contains little or no history, whereas the Bible displays a historical dimension throughout. Furthermore, it includes history no human being could have written, for it includes the very beginning of our universe in Genesis and a description of its end in Revelation. Either this is human imagination, or God himself has revealed it – there are no other explanation.

When we looked at the book of Joshua, we saw how prophetic history is a special type of history because it records events in terms of what God says and does with his people Israel. What we have in the Bible is no ordinary history book, simply recording what a nation has done and experienced – it is God's story of his dealings with his people.

There are four possible levels when it comes to studying history:

1 **The study of personalities**: this approach involves detailed analysis of the individuals who made history – monarchs, military leaders, philosophers, thinkers. Their

lives control what is included; they are the reference point for all that happens.

2 **The study of peoples**: here the focus is on whole nations or people groups. We discover how nations grow stronger and weaker and how this affects the balance of power within the world.

3 **The study of patterns**: aside from the personalities and peoples, this approach looks for the patterns which exist across time frames, such as the way civilizations rise and fall. It is less concerned with the detail and more with themes.

4 **The study of purpose**: historians also ask where history is heading. They look for meaning and purpose. Marxist historians believe in dialectical materialism, i.e. the history of peoples includes conflict, especially between the poor and the ruling classes. Evolutionary optimists believe in the ascent of man, i.e. humanity is making progress to a better world. Others look at war throughout history and predict doom and gloom

The study of purpose can be divided into two strands: on the one hand there are those who see history as linear progression – things are moving forward with the present building on the past; on the other hand there are those who see history as a series of cycles where things tend to come full circle – to them there is little forward progression, just aimless and futile activity signifying nothing.

It is no surprise that a divine view of history includes a sense of purpose. It is not the optimism of the evolutionists, for not everything 'gets better', but biblical history does have a purpose, for God is in control and will bring things to the ending he intends. History is, indeed, 'his story'.

These two aspects of history – the linear and the cyclical views – will help us understand Judges and Ruth. The history in Judges is a classic case of a series of cycles: the same cycle is identified on seven occasions and, although the time line is there, it is largely in the background. Ruth, by contrast, is a time-line story with a beginning, a middle and an end, and a clear sense of progress.

The pattern of history in the book of Judges mirrors accurately the sort of lives many people live when they do not know God. They get up, go to work, come home, watch the television and go to bed again, ready to repeat the same cycle the next day. It is life on a large roundabout! You get nowhere and achieve nothing. The pattern seen in Ruth is more in keeping with the way God intends his people to proceed through life. Here there is purpose and meaning, a movement towards a goal.

The most important thing to establish about any book in the Bible is the reason why it was written. Some books reveal their purpose very easily, but Judges and Ruth require rather more investigation. We will need to examine each book in detail before we can come to any conclusions about the purpose behind them.

Judges

Most people have a Sunday school knowledge of the book of Judges – they only know the 'bowdlerized' version. Thomas Bowdler did not approve of certain parts of William Shakespeare's plays, so he revised them, omitting what he regarded as the 'naughty bits', and now his name has gone down in history. In the same way Sunday school stories from Judges omit some of the less palatable elements – concubines, prostitutes being cut up into pieces, rape, murder, phallic symbols, and so on. As a result many people are familiar with particular personalities within the book, such as Samson, Delilah,

Deborah and Gideon, but have no knowledge of the rest of it, let alone its overall theme and purpose.

Individual stories

The stories within the book are certainly gripping. There is an economy of words, but interesting detail is provided in vivid descriptions which make the characters live for the reader.

The amount of space given to each character is surprisingly varied. Samson has four chapters all to himself, Gideon has three, Deborah and Barak have two, but some have just a short paragraph. It almost seems that the more sensational they were, the more space they were given. Clearly the author's purpose is not to give a balanced account of each hero. It is easy, however, to get the impression that the book is about a series of folk heroes who saved the day in whatever situation they faced (and the book contains a selection of quite bizarre events), rather like Nelson or Wellington in British history.

We read early in the book of Caleb's younger brother **Othniel**. All we are really told is that he brought peace to his people for 40 years.

We read of **Ehud**, the left-handed leader who concealed his 18-inch swordblade by strapping it to his right leg. Since most people were right handed, it was customary to check the left leg for weapons. He was thus able to take his weapon into a private meeting with the King of Moab and plunge it into the King's belly!

We read of **Shamgar**, who killed 600 Philistines with an ox-goad.

We read of **Deborah** and **Barak**. Deborah was a prophetess, married to Lappidoth. Her name means 'Busy bee' and Lappidoth means 'Flash' in Hebrew! Deborah would settle disputes by hearing the answer from the Lord, and on an occasion recorded in Judges she told Barak to lead the people into

battle. Barak refused to go into battle without her. Senior offi-
cers in Israel, then and today, always lead the troops into battle.
God was angry with Barak's refusal and told him that the
enemy Sisera would fall to the hand of a woman in order to
humiliate him. And so it proved.

The next story concerns **Gideon**, one of the most fearful
men in the Bible. He put some meat on an altar and fire from
heaven burned up the meat. Then he asked the Lord for a sign
from heaven, as if the fire was not enough! God graciously
provided a further sign through a fleece which was dry one day
and wet the next. Gideon had to learn that it is by God's
strength and strategy that battles are won. God reduced his
army from 300,000 to 300 so that Gideon would learn not to
put his trust in human resources.

The next character we read of is **Abimelech** (more of him
later); then comes **Tola**, who receives only the brief comment
that he led Israel for 23 years. After him **Jair** led Israel for 22
years and had 30 sons who, we are told, rode 30 donkeys and
controlled 30 towns. A little interesting detail, but nothing more!

There is a longer section recounting the story of **Jephthah**,
the head of Gilead. He made the rash vow that he would sacrifice to the Lord whatever came to meet him when he returned
from battle and ended up having to sacrifice his only daughter.

Ibzan of Bethlehem had 30 daughters and 30 sons who all
married outside the clan of Judah. **Elon** led Israel for 10 years.
Abdon, who came after him, had 40 sons, 30 grandsons and 70
donkeys! Again no more details are given.

When we come to **Samson**, however, we learn far more.
His name literally means 'sunshine'. He was brought up as a
Nazarene, which meant that he was not allowed to take alcohol
or cut his hair. It is an extraordinary tale of a man who had
trouble with women. He married, but his marriage broke up
before the honeymoon. He moved on to a nameless prostitute

before finally joining with a mistress called Delilah. Although having great physical strength, Samson was actually a weak man. His weakness was not primarily his relationships, but stemmed from a weakness of character. His charismatic anointing enabled him to accomplish many amazing feats of strength, but then the Spirit of the Lord departed from him. He was captured by the Philistines, blinded and put on a treadmill, the laughing stock of the Philistines.

Many years ago I preached a sermon called 'Samson's hair is growing again'. It became well known and one young woman who heard it wrote a poem about the blind Samson being led by the little boy to the pillars of the temple, where he pulled the whole temple down.

The boy who held his hand

They gouged them out,
At first
I could not bear to look:
  Empty and raw and cruel.
I would not look:
  The shock of emptiness,
  Knowing that he would not see.
I watched the shaven head bowed low
  Rocking with the rhythm of the grindstone.
  Round. Round. Round.
I watched the needless shackles:
  Heavy and hard,
  Biting the flesh that needs no binding.

Now
It does not matter that his eyes are gone:

I am his eyes,
   He sees through me.
He has to see through me, there is no other way.
And I have wept the tears he cannot weep,
   For all those careless years.
And I have learned to love this broken man,
While he has learned at last to fear his God.

So
I am not afraid to die:
Happy to be his eyes this one last time.
Taking his hand,
Leading with practised care,
Step by guided step
Into the place where he can pray,
'Lord,
O Sovereign Lord.'
And as the pillars fall, I cry
'Amen.'

In his last five minutes Samson did more for his people than he had done in all the years of his life.

HUMAN WEAKNESS

The Bible is always honest about the failings and weaknesses of the individuals it describes and Judges is no exception. The characters in the book reveal a number of flaws: Barak was not manly; Gideon was fearful, constantly asking for signs, and towards the end of his life made a gold ephod, a priestly 'pullover', which later proved to be a 'snare' to Israel, a relic which had become an object of devotion. Jephthah was the son of a prostitute who made a reckless vow; Samson treated his wife poorly, slept with a prostitute and took a mistress. They were not strong characters, nor were they holy people, yet God used them!

DIVINE STRENGTH

How did these less than perfect people manage to achieve so much? It was not through their own power. Their secret was that the Holy Spirit came on them – they were all 'charismatic' people.

Judges gives us vivid examples of divine strength working through weak people, as we read how these individuals were able to perform supernatural feats. Samson was perhaps the most graphic example of this, but there are many amazing stories. This is an especially important point to note, because the anointing of the Holy Spirit only comes on a *few* in the Old Testament. In Judges such anointing was experienced by just 12 people out of the 2 million who populated Israel at that time. We note too that the Holy Spirit comes on them *temporarily*, not permanently: for example, the text states that the Holy Spirit *left* Samson. In the Old Testament it was an anointing Spirit that touched them for a time rather than an indwelling Spirit who stayed with them.

WHAT WERE THE JUDGES?

Our consideration of some of the individual stories of the judges has omitted an important question. What exactly were the judges? Who were they and what did they do?

In English they are called 'judges', but this expression does not really capture the essence of the word originally used to describe them. When we read that Samson 'judged' Israel, or that Gideon 'judged' Israel, the idea behind the Hebrew expression is that they were 'troubleshooters' who saved the people of God from themselves and others. They are never given a title as such, but are described in terms of what they did. Indeed, the only person to whom the noun is applied in the book of Judges is God. He is *the* Judge, sorting out their problems. It would therefore be more correct to say that God is the rescuer or troubleshooter who operates through these heroes, by his Spirit, for the benefit of the people.

They are concerned with justice within the nation, but mainly with external problems, since the people are surrounded by hostile nations who attack them at various times: the Ammonites (three times), the Amalekites (twice), the Moabites (once) , the Midianites (once) and the Philistines (three times). There is also specific mention of the Kings of Jericho, Moab and Hazor.

The people of God had come into a highly populated area, to peoples largely hostile to their presence. They were perceived as invaders. The only justification for them being in that land at all was that God had given it to them, and they were to exact punishment on the resident population by wiping them out. Thus the book is not just about individual heroes – or the study of personalities, the first level of history described at the beginning of this chapter – but whole peoples too – the second level of history.

National history

If you add together all the years that the 12 people mentioned above judged Israel, they come to 400, but the book of Judges actually covers only 200 years. How can this be so?

GEOGRAPHICAL

This problem is easily resolved when we realize what the judges are actually doing. When we read about Gideon and Samson we tend to think that they were delivering the whole nation, but Israel was now divided into groups of tribes, spread over a wide area roughly the size of Wales. Therefore, when we read that a judge ruled for 40 years, it may only apply to tribes in the north. Another judge may have been saving a situation in the south at the same time. Samson, for example, delivered the southern tribes and Gideon the northern ones.

POLITICAL

At this time there was a leadership vacuum within Israel. Moses had led them out of Egypt, Joshua had led them into the Promised Land, but with both these great men dead, there was no figurehead for the nation – bearing in mind that this was before the days of the monarchy. Thus the judges were *local* leaders, commanding the loyalty of groups of tribes, but not uniting the whole nation.

MORAL

There was a moral reason why the tribes were continually facing opposition from other nations and people groups, and this is the heart of the book's message. The structure of the book makes this clear, as we shall see if we look at a brief outline of it. It divides very clearly into three parts.

1. **Inexcusable compromise (1–2)**
   (i) Allowances
   (ii) Alliances

2. **Incorrigible conduct (3–16)**
   (i) Sedition by the people
   (ii) Subjection by an enemy
   (iii) Supplication to the Lord
   (iv) Salvation by a deliverer

3. **Inevitable corruption (17–21)**
   (i) Idolatry in the north – Dan
   (ii) Immorality in the south – Benjamin

In Section 2, the four stages of the cycle are repeated seven times. The book finishes with a statement that has actually been the refrain throughout: 'There was no king in those days, every man did what was right in his own eyes.'

1. Inexcusable compromise

(I) ALLOWANCES – VULNERABLE VALLEYS

God sent Israel into the land to destroy the inhabitants totally. Archaeology confirms the wicked practices of the Canaanite people – sexual diseases were rife. Those who question the justice of this extermination forget God's Word to Abraham about the future of his descendants. He was told that the Jews would stay in Egypt for centuries until the wickedness of the Amorites reached its 'full measure'. God was tolerant of their wickedness, but they finally overstepped the mark and he used Israel as the instrument of his judgement on a most perverted society.

Instead of following God's commands, however, Israel were selective in their punishment. They captured the hills and mountains but allowed many of the peoples to remain, especially those living in the valleys. Israel thus became divided into three groups: northern, central and southern. Communication between the tribes was difficult and they were unable to respond speedily and unitedly when external threats arose. Furthermore, the valleys provided routes for invaders, who were only too keen to exploit such internal weakness.

(II) ALLIANCES – MIXED MARRIAGES

The lax standards of the valleys were too great a temptation for many Israelite men, and before long Israelites had married outside their faith in clear defiance of God's law which forbade 'mixed marriages'. This affected the spiritual life of Israel. If you marry a child of the devil you are bound to have problems with your father-in-law! Any designs on holy living were dashed and many Israelites in unequal marriages ended up serving Canaanite gods. The spiritual influence of the non-believer tends to be stronger in a mixed marriage, even today. The service of Canaanite gods led inevitably to immorality, for wrong belief always leads to wrong behaviour.

2. Incorrigible conduct

The bulk of the book of Judges consists of a series of cycles. With almost monotonous regularity the people of God repeat the same pattern.

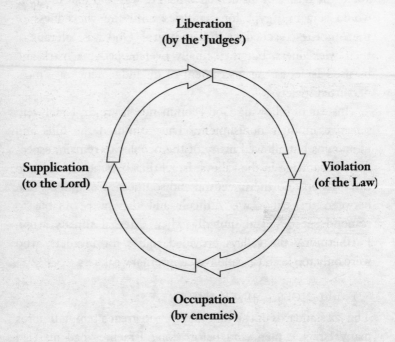

Liberation
(by the 'Judges')

Supplication
(to the Lord)

Violation
(of the Law)

Occupation
(by enemies)

- **Supplication**: It starts with Israel crying out to the Lord because they are facing oppression of some kind.
- **Liberation**: God sends a deliverer (e.g. Gideon, Samson) to rescue the people.
- **Violation**: In spite of their deliverance, the people slip back into sin.
- **Occupation**: God therefore sends a hostile people (e.g. Midianites, Philistines) to overpower Israel. Israel becomes a vassal state in a land they should have been freely owning.
- **Supplication**: In view of the hardship of the situation, they cry out to the Lord again and so the cycle continues. It seems they only pray when they are in trouble. It is hard to tell whether they are truly repentant or merely regretting the consequences of their behaviour. Clearly many were unaware that the oppression was their fault.

The cycle does not just apply to the whole nation: individuals also live in a similar routine of sin and forgiveness and further sin. It is not simply an endless cycle either, but a spiral going downwards. Things get steadily worse.

3. Inevitable corruption

The last part of the book of Judges is a most unedifying account of what happened to the people. There were two situations, one in the north in the territory of Dan and one in the south in the territory of Benjamin. On both occasions, the people of God were misled by a priest. It is a perfect illustration of the maxim mentioned earlier, that idolatry (wrong belief) leads to immorality (wrong behaviour).

(I) IDOLATRY IN THE NORTH – DAN

The story starts with a son, Micah from Ephraim, stealing 1,100 shekels from his own mother. He returns the money to her and she is so delighted that she uses it to make an idol which she gives to Micah for the private shrine he has set up in his home.

A young Levite comes to Micah's house in search of lodgings and is offered the opportunity to be his father and priest for a regular income, clothing and food. He accepts. Later the tribes of Dan, who failed to take the land God allocated to them in the south, migrate north. When their leaders lodge in this house with the idols and the priest, they offer the priest the chance to officiate for their whole tribe, for more money, and he accepts.

In clear violation of the law of God, therefore, the tribe of Dan slips into idolatry. Just as Judas Iscariot, one of the 12 disciples, went missing after his great sin, the tribe of Dan is missing in the book of Revelation. The sin starts with a man who steals money from his mother, then it is carried over to a Levite who becomes a private chaplain, first to a family and then to a whole tribe – without any proper appointment or authorisation.

(II) IMMORALITY IN THE SOUTH – BENJAMIN

This story is even worse. Another Levite from the tribe of Ephraim takes a concubine from Bethlehem in Judah. She leaves him and returns to her family home. After four months the Levite arrives in Bethlehem to seek her return. The father keeps urging the Levite to stay at his home before finally letting her go. They set off too late in the day and only get as far as Jerusalem, a pagan city at that time. The Levite refuses to stay with 'pagans', so they travel north to the tribe of Benjamin, arriving at Gibeah by nightfall. They are offered hospitality by an old man who welcomes them into his home. However, while they are eating, they are interrupted by 'wicked men of the city' who demand that the newcomer be given to them for sex. The old man refuses, but offers instead his daughter. Eventually the Levite gives them his concubine. The next morning the concubine lies dead on the doorstep, having been gang-raped through the night.

The Levite cuts his concubine up into 12 pieces and sends them to the other tribes of Israel. When the Israelites discover that men of the tribe of Benjamin committed the crime, they seek revenge on the perpetrators. The Benjaminites are offended by the accusation and refuse to hand the men over.

A civil war results which almost wipes out the tribe – only 600 men are left. Their towns are destroyed and all the women and children are slaughtered. The other tribes had vowed not to give their daughters in marriage to the tribe of Benjamin, but now the tribe is on the brink of extinction and the Israelites have pity on them and take action to prevent this happening. They find 400 virgins from Jabesh Gilead as wives for the Benjaminites, but they need more. They then concoct a clever plan. They hold a festival at Shiloh and allow the Benjaminites to kidnap their daughters – thus not technically 'giving' them away and so fulfilling the letter if not the spirit of their previous oath.

It is a dreadful tale in all aspects and, alongside the story of the tribe of Dan, it makes a depressing end to the book of Judges.

Theological or eternal purpose

After such a gloomy story we turn to a more uplifting subject: a consideration of the theological purpose of the book. Ultimately Bible history is not a human record but a record of what God has said and done, showing us who he is.

We have noted already that God is the judge or deliverer of the people, since he is the only person to whom the noun 'judge' is applied in the book. He is the real hero, and success is achieved when the human leaders co-operate with him.

However, when we ask the question, 'Who drove the Canaanites from the land, Israel or God?' we must reply, 'Both!' We can sum up the situation like this: Without him they could not; without them he would not. On the one hand God declared that he would give them the land and drive out the inhabitants, but on the other hand he needed Israel to respond to his direction.

Furthermore, we read that in some cases God did not drive out the opposition, but left them in the land to test Israel and teach them to fight. We learn from Amos that just as God brought Israel out of Egypt, he brought the Philistines from Crete as neighbours, to inflict injury on Israel.

Within the book of Judges, therefore, we find that God chastises his people. He delivers them *to* evil, demonstrating his justice, as well as *from* evil, showing his mercy.

This principle is also seen in the New Testament. There is, of course, the line in the Lord's Prayer: 'Lead us not into temptation but deliver us from evil.' The power of the Holy Spirit can heal the sick, but it can also bring disease; it can give sight to the blind, but it can also prevent good eyes from seeing; it can raise the dead, but it brings death too, as with Ananias and Sapphira. The ultimate sanction in church discipline is to hand over erring members to Satan, whose destructive power over the body may bring them to their senses and save their souls on the day of judgement.

Yet at the same time God hears the prayers of Israel and responds. He is grieved by their misery, he is patient and faithful, in spite of the people's repeated disobedience. So we read how God answered prayer, sending anointed leaders and directing operations, for example with Gideon and Barak. We see a dynamic relationship between God and man, each affecting the other.

Noting this important dynamic still does not explain the purpose of the book, however, but this will not become truly clear until we have looked at Ruth as well. At this stage all we see is the unedifying cycle of Israel getting into and out of trouble. We do not yet know where it is going.

The reasons for these problems within Israel can be explained in two ways:

1. SECOND-GENERATION MEMBERS

The people of Israel now occupying the Promised Land did not have the same knowledge of God and what he had done for them as the previous generation. They did not want to know God. Instead they did what was right in their own eyes, but wrong in his eyes. Everyone was a law to himself.

2. SECOND-GENERATION LEADERS

There was no seamless succession in the leadership. When a judge died, there was a gap before another judge appeared, and during this gap the people reverted to the type of behaviour which led to God's punishment. The pattern of the cycle is indicated by phrases such as, 'as long as the judge lived … but when the judge died…' This was very different from the dynastic succession which prevailed in other nations, ensuring continuity and stability – and the judges only ruled over a limited group, not a united nation.

This question of kingship crops up a number of times.

1 **Gideon** is offered the throne by his followers following his victory over the Midianites. The people ask him to start a dynasty. Some argue that he should have accepted, but clearly this is not God's time for a king to be chosen. Gideon tells the people their problem is that they have not looked to God as their king.

2 Following Gideon the leadership is in the hands of a number of people. **Abimelech** asks the people whether they

would prefer his sole leadership to leadership by Gideon's 70 sons as a group. He is duly installed and proceeds to murder his brothers. Things get steadily worse as his hunger for power demonstrates that he has little interest in the welfare of the people, and he is eventually killed in battle.

3 Throughout Judges we read the refrain, '**There was no king in those days**…' and the suggestion is that things would have been much better if there had been one.

We will return to this theme later. For now the important point to note is that Judges tells us there is a desperate need for a king. As we turn to the book of Ruth we are faced with the more positive message that a king will be provided. Ruth starts to address the question, 'Who will it be?'

Ruth

The book of Ruth was written at the same time as Judges but there could hardly be a greater contrast between the two.

- Judges includes the stories of many people, Ruth just a few.
- Judges is relatively large, while Ruth is one of the smallest Old Testament books.
- Judges covers the whole of Israel, Ruth just one small town.
- Judges spans 200 years, Ruth just one generation.

Ruth reads like a Thomas Hardy novel, with the sort of romance which would not be out of place in a magazine story. It is a breath of fresh air after Judges. In Judges we have mass killing, rape, a prostitute cut up into pieces, civil war, evil priests. It is just two miles from the Benjaminites' territory to Judah where Ruth is located, but it is a totally different atmosphere.

Ruth is only four chapters long. The first two chapters are about two inseparable women, and the second two chapters are about two influential men. These four people form the main characters in the drama.

1 Mother-in-law's loss
2 Daughter-in-law's loyalty
3 Redeemer kinsman's love
4 Royal king's line

1. Mother-in-law's loss

The story begins with a famine in Israel, which caused two men to leave for Moab. We can guess that the famine was a punishment from God, for this was a common sign of God's displeasure, and it provides a contrast with the location of the main drama – Bethlehem means 'house of bread' in Hebrew.

If the family had learned the lessons from Israel's history, they would have known that searching for food outside Israel always led to problems, as the stories of Abraham, Isaac and Jacob testify, but there is no record that they prayed to God for food. So Naomi and her husband travelled east across the hills on the far side of the Dead Sea to Moab. As time passed each of their two sons married a Moabite woman. Things went from bad to worse. Naomi's husband died and the two sons died also. The three widows were left alone. In those days a widow's future was bleak. The whole drama started from the men's refusal to rely on God. They sought a human solution to their situation instead of asking God what was happening and what they should do.

God would have told them that the famine was part of his punishment, and if only they would turn back to him they would have enough food again. But they did not even wait to ask him, let alone listen for an answer.

As a result of this crisis Naomi became bitter. Her name actually means 'pleasure', but when she returned to Israel she was unrecognizable to her old relatives and asked to be called 'Mara', meaning 'bitter', instead. She encouraged her two daughters-in-law to stay in Moab, knowing that returning to Judah would mean little prospect of remarrying. The men in Judah were not likely to marry outside their clan.

Orpah agreed and went back to Moab and is never heard of again. On the basis of her choice she had no more place in God's purpose. Ruth, however, went with Naomi and her name has gone down in history as an ancestor of Our Lord Jesus Christ.

The story carries the reminder that much can hang on just one decision. It is the choices we take that make up our character, and Ruth made the right choice at the right time.

At last we see someone whose actions break out of the endless cycle. Ruth became part of God's line instead. Her name is mentioned in the genealogy of Jesus in Matthew, despite the fact that she was both a Gentile and a woman.

2. Daughter-in-law's loyalty

Ruth was a beautiful character, both inside and out. She was full of humility and yet she had the sort of boldness that men find attractive. She was loyal, with a serving spirit, but she was not passive or an underdog by any means.

She not only chose to stay with Naomi, but chose Naomi's people and Naomi's God. God was evidently real to her, even though she had seen him punishing his people. On four occasions she said 'I will' to Naomi. In being so loyal to Naomi she demonstrated her love for her. 'Loyalty' and 'love' are almost the same word in Hebrew. Love that is not loyal is not true love. Likewise, God's covenant love for his people means that he sticks with them through thick and thin.

Furthermore, we read that Ruth found 'favour' in the eyes of the Lord. In Hebrew, 'favour' is the same word as 'favourite' – she became one of God's favourites. It is clear from the story that Ruth became the talk of the town in Bethlehem, for the Lord did not stop showing his kindness to Ruth.

3. Redeemer kinsman's love

The second half of the book includes two influential men, Boaz and the man who would become king.

Boaz was a man of great standing and great generosity. It was common for the poor to be allowed to collect any grain remaining in the field after harvest, but Boaz instructed his workers to make sure that Ruth especially received a large provision.

There are two other customs in the book of Ruth which we must appreciate in order to understand the unfolding drama. The first is the Levirate marriage. In the year of Jubilee, every 50 years, all the property was returned to the original family that owned it in the previous Jubilee year. It was imperative, therefore, that there was a male family representative to claim the property after 50 years. The Levirate law stated that if a woman's husband died before she had a son to pass on her inheritance, her husband's brother had to marry her and give her a son, thus keeping the property in the family. Ruth, of course, had been married to someone who was entitled to property, but now she had no husband or son, so a relative was under the obligation to marry her to keep her husband's name and line going and reinherit the property when it became available in Jubilee year.

The second law to understand was a social custom. A girl could not propose marriage to a man in those days, but she was free to indicate that she would like to be married to someone and could do that in a number of ways. One was to warm the man's feet! So when Ruth lay at Boaz's feet and covered them with her cloak she was indicating that she would not mind being married to him. These two customs explain how Boaz married Ruth.

When Ruth lay at Boaz's feet, it was a clear sign that she was interested. He was flattered that she had chosen him, as he was neither the oldest nor the youngest kinsman she could have chosen. However, his older brother was the one who should fulfil the legal duty, so he had to give him first option! His older brother gave his consent in the customary way, taking off his sandal and giving it to Boaz – the equivalent of shaking hands on a deal. Ruth and Boaz were free to marry.

4. Royal king's line

It is a beautiful story – a lovely rural romance. But we must ask what God was doing behind all this, for it is unlikely that the story would be included in Scripture merely as a light interlude. It becomes clear that God was preparing a royal line for a king of Israel. Ruth's right choice in joining with Naomi and returning to be part of her people was part of God's right choice, for he had chosen her to be part of the royal line.

Indeed, although God is not directly identified as being involved in the drama, he is frequently mentioned in the book, as the characters ask him to bless others. Naomi asked the Lord to bless Ruth for being with her. The harvesters asked God to bless Boaz and he returned the blessing to them. Boaz asked the Lord to bless Ruth for choosing him. When they spoke of God they used God's name, YAHWEH, a name which functions like 'always' in English – God is 'always' my provider, 'always' at my side, 'always' my healer.

It is interesting to note that Boaz was a direct descendent of Judah, one of the 12 sons of Jacob. He was also a descendant of Tamar, who had offspring after she was raped, which shows that God can use the most unlikely situations as part of his plan. Jacob gave a prophecy to Judah on his deathbed: 'The sceptre will not depart from Judah nor the ruler's staff from between his feet until he comes to whom it belongs.' This was several centuries before they thought of having a king, and yet Jacob promised Judah that a royal line would come from his house.

We learn too that Boaz's grandmother was not a Jew. Rahab the prostitute was the first Gentile in the land of Canaan to embrace the God of Israel. So we have a mixed family tree: Tamar was raped, Rahab was a Gentile and a prostitute, Ruth was a Moabite. And yet these are all ancestors of our Lord Jesus Christ.

Who wrote Judges and Ruth?

It is time now to examine why Judges and Ruth belong together, and also to answer the question: Who wrote them and why?

The end of a book of the Bible often reveals its purpose. The phrase, 'There was no king in Israel *in those days*' means that the book of Judges, and therefore Ruth as well, was written *after* they were led by a king. It is also obvious from the end of Ruth that David was not the king at the time of writing, for we read, 'Jesse was the father of David,' not 'Jesse was the father of David the King.'

These two facts strongly suggest that the book was written when there was a king, but before David's time. The only period when this was the case was when Saul was king, since David was king directly after Saul. So the book was written when Saul, the first king of Israel, was on the throne, the people's choice. He was chosen for his height and his physical appearance – not for his character or ability.

If we know when the book was written, we can also ask who wrote it. The speeches of the prophet Samuel in the first book of Samuel have been found to be identical in language to the book of Judges and Ruth. And it was his style to teach from the history of his people. It is most likely, therefore, that Samuel wrote Judges and Ruth as one book, when Saul was king.

More of the purpose for writing can be discerned when we ask which tribe King Saul came from. The answer is Benjamin. The whole message of the two books is that Benjamin is bad stock, in contrast to Judah and those in Bethlehem. In other words, the two-volume work was written to prepare the people to switch from Saul to David. Samuel had secretly anointed David but needed to prepare the people to accept him as king rather than their own choice of Saul.

He asks his readers to compare the degraded men of Benjamin with the delightful people in Bethlehem. At the very end Samuel mentions that Jesse was the father of David, knowing that he was God's appointed king and was going to change the whole situation.

This theory is backed up by a detail included in the first chapter of Judges. When the tribe of Judah entered the Promised Land the city of Jerusalem was assigned to the tribe of Benjamin. But the early part of Judges tells us that the city was in the hands of the Jebusites 'to this day', implying that Benjamin never conquered it. One of David's first acts as king, recorded in 1 Samuel, was to capture the city. This provides further clarification for the date of the book and confirms the likelihood that its purpose was to encourage people to be pro-David. The position of Ruth alongside Judges brings two cities into view: Bethlehem, the 'house of bread', David's home town, and Jerusalem, occupied by the Jebusites but soon to become the nation's capital.

How can we use Judges and Ruth today?

In the New Testament the apostle Paul tells Timothy that all Scripture is God-breathed and able to make us 'wise for salvation'. Jesus says that the Scriptures bear witness to him, so we must ask how a Christian should read Judges and Ruth.

Judges

Individual Christians can learn a great deal from the characters in the book of Judges. We can learn from the mistakes the judges made as well as from their correct choices. Each story has value to any believer. But we do not look to the judges to provide role models. Indeed, the New Testament discourages such a course. In Hebrews 12 we are told that those who have gone before, described in chapter 11 and including some of these judges, are watching to see how *we* run the race, looking to our only true model in Jesus, the author and perfecter of our faith, whose work of deliverance stands for all time.

The Church needs to study Judges because it could fall into the same spiral of anarchy today, doing what it feels is right in its own eyes. It could fall into error by looking for a visible 'monarchy', a human being whose viewpoint or leadership is valued more than that of Christ. Rule by democracy, oligarchy or autocracy depends on human leaders, but the Bible teaches that we should be led by a theocracy. Our leader is both human and divine; he was on earth and is now in heaven.

We must also remember that God is the same in character today as he was at the time of the events described in Judges and Ruth. He loves his people, and shows this by disciplining those who wander from his path. At the same time he works out his plans for our good. We need not be part of a cycle of despair. We can know real direction and follow God's purposes.

Ruth

Ruth was one of the earliest Gentiles to embrace the God of Israel. She is a picture of all believers who are in the royal line, brothers of Jesus through faith in him.

The book reminds us of Jesus, for if the Church is like Ruth, Boaz is like Christ – the kinsman redeemer. The Church has been brought into the line of the Old Testament people of God. We are the bride and he is the bridegroom. Ruth is not an isolated Old Testament book, but covers a theme which runs throughout the Bible. The whole Bible is a romance, finishing with the wedding supper of the Lamb in the book of Revelation. The Ruth–Boaz romance is a perfect picture of Christ and his Gentile bride.

PART III

1 AND 2 SAMUEL

Introduction

The books which make up 1 and 2 Samuel in the English Bible are just one book in the Jewish Scriptures, and are included as part of the 'former prophets' section. Samuel covers 150 years of history, told from a prophetic point of view to record how God sees things and what he regards as important. The book is named after the prophet who dominates the story, and who probably wrote most of it. It covers great changes in Israel's history and the emergence of the great King David, whose fame is remembered to this day.

Context

Abraham, the father of the Jews, lived around 2000 BC; King David came to the throne around 1000 BC. God's promise to Abraham that he would have descendants and a land is therefore 1,000 years old when we reach the book of Samuel and the arrival of David. According to the Old Testament time chart given earlier in the Overview section (page 7), the book of Samuel records a third change in the pattern of leadership during the history of the people of Israel.

1 **From 2000 to 1500** BC Israel was led by *patriarchs*: Abraham, Isaac, Jacob and Joseph (though they were not a nation at this point).

2 **From 1500 to 1000** BC they were led by *prophets*: Moses through to Samuel.

3 **From 1000 to 500** BC they were led by *princes* (or kings): Saul through to Zedekiah.

4 **In the 500 years leading up to the time of Christ** they were led by *priests*: Joshua through to Annas and Caiaphas.

The dates are approximate, but this gives a helpful summary. Samuel describes the change from prophets to princes (or kings), the 150 years of the upward rise to the empire of David.

It is a highly significant period of Israel's history. The Jews speak of David's reign as the golden era of peace and prosperity when they conquered all the land God had promised them. Even now, Jews long for a renewal of the days when a king reigned over a united and victorious nation. But it was not all good news, and we see in Samuel the beginning of a decline which continues through 1 and 2 Kings until Israel loses everything they gained in the previous 1,000 years.

Before examining how we should interpret them, we will look at the detail of the main stories in the books of Samuel, beginning with an overview of the content and structure.

Structure

1. **Samuel – last judge**
   (i) Hannah – anxious wife
   (ii) Eli – ailing priest
   (iii) Israel – arrogant army
   (iv) Saul – anointed king

2. **Saul – first king**
   (i) Jonathan – adventurous son
   (ii) Samuel – angry prophet
   (iii) David – apparent rival
       IN
       (a) Simple shepherd
       (b) Skilled musician
       (c) Superb warrior
       OUT
       (a) Suspected courtier
       (b) Stalked outlaw
       (c) Soldiering exile
   (iv) Philistines – aggressive foe

3. **David – best king**
   (i) Triumphant ascent
       UP
       (a) Single tribe
       (b) Settled nation
       (c) Sizeable empire
   (ii) Tragic descent
       DOWN
       (a) Disgraced man
       (b) Disintegrated family
       (c) Discontented people

4. **Epilogue**

In this structural chart, the lives of Samuel and Saul are each described in terms of their relationship with three individuals and one people group: Samuel with Hannah, Eli, Saul and Israel; Saul with Jonathan, Samuel, David and the Philistines.

David's life can be summarized very simply in four directional words, as the chart shows: in, out, up, down. The 'in' and 'out' refer to his changing favour with King Saul, the 'up' refers to his move towards the pinnacle of his power as king, and 'down' refers to his journey into the depths of despair.

Content

1. Samuel – last judge

(I) HANNAH – ANXIOUS WIFE

The book begins with the story of Samuel's mother, Hannah. Her husband, Elkanah, has two wives and Hannah, who is childless, has to bear the taunts of the other wife, Peninnah, who does have children. Years pass and Hannah's grief at her childlessness deepens. She visits the temple at Shiloh (where Israel kept the ark of the covenant) and prays that if God will at last grant her a son she will dedicate him to God's service. Eli the priest notices that she is muttering aloud and suspects that she is drunk. Hannah explains that she is deeply troubled and Eli sends her away with God's blessing. Later Hannah conceives and gives birth to a son, whom she names Samuel.

In gratitude she fufils her vow to the Lord and presents Samuel to Eli to serve at the temple. Hannah prays again, reflecting her confidence and joy in God. This prayer is clearly recalled by Mary 1,000 years later, when the angel tells her she is to give birth to Jesus. Her joy and praise in what is now called 'The Magnificat' contains echoes of Hannah's.

(II) ELI – AILING PRIEST

Samuel ministers under the priest, Eli. One night he hears a voice and runs to Eli, assuming that he is calling him, but Eli says he is not. This happens three times before the priest realizes that it is God who wants to speak to Samuel. It is a significant moment, since the prophetic revelation, both verbal and visual, was rare in those days.

Thus Samuel, aged 12, is given the responsibility of telling Eli that God will act in judgement upon his family because his two boys are misbehaving badly and Eli has been turning a blind eye. The sons have been abusing their positions of responsibility, eating consecrated meat and sleeping with some of the women who bring offerings. From then on, God says, no one in Eli's line will see old age.

This encounter was the start of Samuel's prophetic ministry, and it was not the last time that the word he gave would be hard to receive.

(III) ISRAEL – ARROGANT ARMY

The next story concerns Israel's defeat at the hands of the Philistines, the warring nation living on the west coast. The Israelites assume that they lost the battle because they left the ark of the covenant in the temple. Next time, therefore, they take it with them into battle, but are again heavily defeated, with 30,000 foot soldiers killed, including Eli's sons (thus fulfilling the prophecy concerning their early deaths). The ark is captured by the Philistines and taken to the temple of Dagon, the Philistines' god.

On hearing this news, Eli – an old, frail man by this time – falls backwards off his chair and breaks his neck. The ark, however, spells trouble for the Philistines. God sends terrible illnesses upon them and they finally send it back to the Israelites on a cart pulled by two cows. The Philistines follow the cart to see where it goes, and they see it heading uphill in the direction of Jerusalem.

Samuel gathers the Israelites at Mizpah and tells them that the previous defeats have nothing to do with the ark and everything to do with the pagan gods they are worshipping. Israel burns the idols, and this time is victorious in the fight against the Philistines. This demonstrates a principle described in Judges: whenever the Israelites disobey God an enemy comes to defeat them, but whenever they repent and put things right they defeat their enemies.

Samuel's fame grows from this time onwards, and his work as a judge and a prophet becomes greatly valued.

(IV) SAUL – ANOINTED KING

The last public thing that Samuel does as a prophet is to anoint Saul as king. The people ask Samuel whether they can have a king like the nations around them. They know that God is their king, but they want a king who is visible. At first Samuel is offended by their request, until God reminds him that he has no right to take offence, for it is God they have rejected.

God tells Samuel that if the nation has a king, they need to be prepared for the consequences. A king will want a palace and an army, so taxation and conscription will swiftly follow the coronation. In spite of these warnings, the Israelites still insist they want a king and they choose Saul, a man who is taller and more handsome than anybody else.

2. Saul – first king

Saul's anointing takes place secretly. God tells Samuel that the one to be anointed as king will be a man searching for donkeys! So when Saul comes to his home asking for help Samuel knows what to do. Saul is given the gift of prophecy as a sign that he is the heir – though we have few details about what form this took. The people confirm Saul as king, aged 30, and Samuel, the last judge, hands over the leadership.

Saul makes a good start. The people are pleased with his appointment and he experiences early success in defeating the

Ammonites. But it is with respect to his relationships that things soon start to go wrong.

(I) JONATHAN – ADVENTUROUS SON

Saul's son Jonathan is instrumental in defeating the Philistines and Saul is initially very proud of him. Jonathan, however, makes the mistake of going into the next battle without telling his father. He wins, but Saul is jealous of his success and his relationship with Jonathan comes under strain.

In the next story, they are in battle again and Saul makes the rash vow that anyone found eating that day, before he has avenged himself on his enemy, will be put to death. Jonathan, ignorant of the vow, eats some honey. Thus we have the bizarre situation of Saul threatening to kill his own son for disobeying some instructions he did not hear. If the men under his command had not intervened, Jonathan would have lost his life.

(II) SAMUEL – ANGRY PROPHET

Saul's relationship with Samuel also deteriorates. As prophet, Samuel's job is to pass on to Saul the words God gives him. On one occasion Saul is instructed to await Samuel's arrival before offering the post-battle sacrifice. When Samuel is late arriving at the battlefield, Saul conducts the sacrifice himself. Enraged at this arrogant action, Samuel tells him his kingdom is about to be handed to someone else.

Saul's second major error also concerns disobedience to God's word. This time he is commanded to wipe out the Amalekites and their livestock, but Saul spares the king, Agag, and the best of the livestock. Once again Samuel arrives on the scene and finds that Saul has failed to obey all that God has said. Samuel becomes very angry, executes Agag before the altar of the Lord, and tells Saul that to obey is better than to sacrifice. Samuel further tells Saul that because he has rejected the word of the Lord, God has rejected him as king. From that day until Samuel's death, Saul would never hear from Samuel again. The story is a salutary reminder that ritual is no substitute for righteousness. It certainly marked the beginning of the end for the first king of Israel.

Deprived of Samuel's counsel, Saul has no way of finding out the Lord's will and so has no idea whether Israel's battles will be successful or not. Although he pleased God at the beginning of his reign by banning every medium from the land of Israel, at the very end of his reign, some time after Samuel's death, he manages to find one at Endor who is still in business. Saul goes to her and calls up Samuel's spirit for a final conversation. He is told that the imminent battle with the Philistines will be his last.

(III) DAVID – APPARENT RIVAL

Saul's story slips into the background with the arrival of David. The young David enters Saul's service, and we are told that Saul likes him very much, but after a good start Saul's relationship with David goes the way of Jonathan's and Samuel's.

IN

(a) Simple shepherd

David's arrival on the scene comes after God's rejection of Saul as king – although Saul is to remain king for some time. Samuel is sent to David's family home to anoint one of Jesse's sons as king, but finds that none receive God's approval. Only when the eighth and youngest son is called from the field does God indicate that this is the one who will be the next king. David is anointed secretly, pending the time many years later when he will eventually be crowned.

(b) Skilled musician

By this time Saul is deteriorating mentally as well as morally. We read that the Holy Spirit leaves him and an unclean spirit takes over. Saul becomes unpredictable, a man who can fly off the handle without a moment's notice. His advisors find that the one thing that can calm him down is music, so David, known as a skilled harp player, is brought to court and his music soothes Saul's spirit.

(c) Superb warrior

The story of David and Goliath is one of the best known in the Bible. It was the mismatch of the century, the sort of story Jews love: Goliath of Gath was 9 foot 6 inches tall, and David was just a little shepherd boy. It was customary for opposing armies to choose a champion each, who would fight each other. Whoever won would win victory for his side, which saved a lot of bloodshed.

By this stage in the story Saul has abdicated his own role as 'champion' for the nation and so, after some discussion, he allows David to fight Goliath on behalf of Israel. Despite the odds, David is convinced God will give him victory. He believes the battle is the Lord's and that his victory will show the whole world his power. He uses a sling, just as he had in his shepherd's work, and with just one stone from the five he has picked, Goliath is dead and the Philistines routed.

OUT

(a) Suspected courtier

If Saul could be jealous of his own son, what would he make of this new hero? He hears the people singing of how Saul had killed thousands, but David tens of thousands. David becomes a great national hero and Saul comes to hate him. From then on David's life is in danger. David continues to play music to soothe Saul's troubled mind, but there are times when Saul is so enraged that he flings a spear in David's direction.

Later Saul plots to kill him, first by offering him his daughter Merab in marriage in exchange for the defeat of the Philistines. David refuses to accept his daughter and Saul's plans are foiled when David defeats the Philistines unscathed. Later David does marry Michal, another of Saul's daughters.

Saul then asks Jonathan to be involved in David's death, but Jonathan and Michal are on David's side, and in the course of several plots warn him of Saul's intentions.

(b) Stalked outlaw

It becomes clear that David has to leave the palace, so he escapes and hides at Samuel's home in Ramah. Then comes an extraordinary event as Saul and his men try to take David prisoner, but the Spirit of the Lord comes upon them and they prophesy, unable to carry out the plan.

Jonathan continues to help David and they make a covenant whereby Jonathan promises to be David's subject, despite being Saul's son. He is a prince abdicating in favour of a shepherd boy. The Bible depicts a remarkable friendship. We are told that there had never been such love between two men as there was between David and Jonathan.

The priest Ahimelech at Nob feeds David with consecrated bread and gives him Goliath's sword. He flees west to Gath, where he is recognized by the Philistine king as the heir apparent and has to feign insanity in order to escape with his life.

At Adullam some 400 malcontents join with David. He sends his parents into Moab, the home of his great-grandmother for protection, and is told by a prophet to return to Judah.

While he is chasing David in the desert of En-gedi, Saul enters a cave to relieve himself, unaware that David is inside. David cuts off the bottom of his robe and when Saul leaves he shouts after him. Saul is so shaken when he realizes that David could have killed him in the cave that he repents temporarily. But before long the chase resumes.

In the desert of Maon David meets a woman he later marries. Nabal refuses hospitality to David and his men. His wife Abigail, however, brings food to them and saves her family from David's retribution. Nabal dies soon after this and David takes Abigail to be his wife.

(c) Soldiering exile

The most extraordinary part of David's story is one that is not often taught. David becomes fearful that Saul will eventually catch up with him, and so offers himself and his men as mercenaries to the Philistines, Israel's greatest enemy. Before long they become trusted allies.

(IV) PHILISTINES – AGGRESSIVE FOE

Saul's end comes when Israel fights the Philistines. Although David and his men are mercenaries with the Philistines, the Philistine leaders leave them out of this particular battle, concerned that David and his men may not remain loyal to them if they are sent into battle against their own people. In the event they are not needed anyway. The Israelites are heavily defeated, and Saul and Jonathan are killed just as Samuel predicted. The injured Saul falls on his own sword when he realizes his life is ebbing away. Thus the book of 1 Samuel finishes with the death of one of the most enigmatic characters in the whole Bible.

3. David – best king

(I) TRIUMPHANT ASCENT

UP

(a) Single tribe

We see the triumphant ascent of David in the first nine chapters of 2 Samuel. It begins with a lament at the death of Saul and Jonathan, which includes some moving words remembering the warmth of the loving friendship David had known with Jonathan.

There is, however, a war developing between David's house and Saul's house, with tales of murder and revenge abounding. Saul's chief commander Abner changes sides and brings Benjamin with him, but the nation is nonetheless torn apart.

(b) Settled nation

The tribe of Judah crowns David as king in Hebron in the south, where he remains for seven years. He eventually settles the nation as one unit, helped in part by the capture of Jerusalem from the hands of the Jebusites. The Jebusites are convinced that Jerusalem is safe from attack, but David takes the city by entering it via a staircase that runs from inside the city to a spring outside the walls.

It is worth noting that not only did Jerusalem have excellent fortifications for a capital city, with cliffs on three of its four sides, but it was also on 'neutral' territory between Judah (the tribe who supported David) and Benjamin (Saul's tribe). It was thus an appropriate political capital as neither Judah nor Benjamin could claim it was theirs.

(c) Sizeable empire

The book proceeds to chart David's successful campaigns against the Philistines, the Ammonites and the Edomites, whose lands became part of a vast empire. For the first (and last) time, all the land God had promised was in Israel's hands. Israel was at the peak of her history.

Even at such a time of personal success, however, David is keen to remember Saul's house, and he honours Mephi-bosheth, the lame son of Jonathan, crippled in both feet.

(II) TRAGIC DESCENT

DOWN

(a) Disgraced man

David's decline begins one fateful afternoon. The army is away fighting against Ammon and David, who should be leading them, is at home looking out of a palace window. He notices Bathsheba, the wife of his next-door neighbour, bathing on the roof and likes what he sees. He proceeds to break five of the Ten Commandments. He covets his neighbour's wife, he bears false witness against the husband, he steals the wife, he com-mits adultery with her, and finally he arranges the murder of the husband. It is a terrible story and from that afternoon the nation goes downhill. Over the next 500 years they lose every-thing that God gave them.

Bathsheba becomes pregnant, David seeks to cover it up and eventually arranges for Uriah her husband to be killed in battle. The baby dies and David takes Bathsheba into the palace as his wife. She becomes pregnant again, but this baby survives and is called Solomon (meaning 'peace'). But David has no peace. A year later God sends the prophet Nathan to David to tell him of his sin through a parable and David real-izes the gravity of his sin. Psalm 51 is a prayer of confession following this revelation.

(b) Disintegrated family

It seems as if David's immoral behaviour becomes a catalyst for unpleasantness throughout the family. His eldest son Amnon rapes Tamar, one of his sisters. David's second son Absalom hears what happened and two years later exacts his own revenge.

Absalom gains such popularity with the people that David is obliged to leave Jerusalem. Once again he finds himself in exile.

In accordance with a prophecy made by Nathan, Absalom parades David's wives on the palace roof and has sex with them in public. A subsequent battle leads to the death of Absalom, but David is distraught, wishing that he had died instead.

(c) Discontented people

The rancour within David's family affects the people as a whole. Despite the vast empire they now control, they are not happy with David's leadership. The capital is in the south and the people in the north feel neglected. Concerns are brought to a head by a Benjaminite, Sheba, who refuses to recognize David as king and starts a revolt. David quells the uprising, but the feelings of anger remain.

4. Epilogue

The last chapters are arranged using a literary device, with the contents of the epilogue set out according to corresponding themes. The structure can be broken down into six sections, labelled A1, B1, C1, C2, B2, A2, and the sections A1 and A2, B1 and B2, and C1 and C2 cover similar themes.

A1 LEGACY FROM THE PAST

The whole of Israel faces a famine for three years. God tells David that the famine is a punishment on Israel for Saul's earlier slaughter of the Gibeonites, a group whom the Israelites had vowed not to touch. The Gibeonites request the death of seven of Saul's descendants as recompense for this outrage and David hands them over.

B1 DAVID'S MEN

There is a short account of David's 'giant killers' – the men who fought alongside him and gave him victory over the Philistines in a series of battles.

C1 DAVID'S PSALM

One of David's greatest psalms records how God delivered him from all his enemies. He writes of God as his rock, his fortress and his deliverer – the words of a man who can look back on God's extraordinary provision throughout his life and give thanks for it.

C2 THE LAST WORDS OF DAVID

These sayings read like a psalm as David reflects on God's Spirit, who inspired his writing of the songs which have been sung down through the ages and are perhaps David's greatest legacy.

B2 MORE CITATIONS FOR BRAVERY

David recognizes, records and honours the men who fought with him, including the three who crept back to Bethlehem to bring David some water when he was on the run.

A2 DIVINE JUDGEMENT AGAIN FALLS ON ISRAEL

At the end of his life, David is tempted by Satan to conduct a census of the fighting men of Israel. His motivation is pride and God punishes his action. Gad the prophet is sent to convey God's displeasure and David has three options: three years of famine, three months of fleeing from enemies, or three days of plague. He opts for the third and 70,000 people die of the plague.

David cries out to the Lord to stop the plague and is told to sacrifice at the threshing floor of Araunah the Jebusite, a flat area high above the city of Jerusalem. He offers a sacrifice and the plague stops. David sees the threshing floor as an ideal place to build a temple for God. He is offered the land free, but David says his offering to the Lord would be unworthy if it cost him nothing and insists on buying the land. The books of Kings describe the building of the temple on this very spot.

David was not allowed to build the temple himself because God said he had 'blood on his hands'. The temple had to be built by a man of peace. So the temple in Jerusalem, which means 'city of peace', was built by David's son Solomon. Although David drew up the plans, arranged the workmen and collected the materials, it was his son Solomon who saw the project through.

How should we read Samuel?

Our overview of Samuel has so far omitted any mention of how we should read the book. All readers approach the text with certain expectations, but it is important that we read the Bible as it was intended to be read if we are to understand and interpret it correctly. Samuel is no exception. There are six different levels at which we can read any series of Bible stories and it is important to choose the right one.

1. **Anecdotal (interesting stories)**
    (i) Children
    (ii) Adults

2. **Existential (personal messages)**
    (i) Guidance
    (ii) Comfort

3. **Biographical (character studies)**
   (i) Individual
   (ii) Social

4. **Historical (national development)**
   (i) Leadership
   (ii) Structure

5. **Critical (possible errors)**
   (i) 'Lower' criticism
   (ii) 'Higher' criticism

6. **Theological (providential over-ruling)**
   (i) Justice – retribution
   (ii) Mercy – redemption

1. Anecdotal

(I) CHILDREN

The simplest way is to focus on the most interesting stories. Sunday school teachers select the events that will communicate best with the children, and the story of David and Goliath, for example, is a particular favourite.

Maria Matilda Penstone expressed it like this:

God has given us a book full of stories
which was made for his people of old.
It begins with a tale of a garden
and finishes with the city of gold.
There are stories for parents and children,
for the old who are ready to rest,
but for all who can read them or listen
the story of Jesus is best.

There is some merit in using the stories in this way, but it is selective. Teachers can easily distort the true meaning of an event in favour of a platitude which they feel is of value and on a level which they think the children will understand.

(II) ADULTS

The stories in Samuel are superbly told, with an economy of words and a beautiful style. Since adults also enjoy a good story, many read the Bible purely for its anecdotal value. Film directors have enjoyed adapting stories such as David and Bathsheba for the silver screen.

While it is good that the stories are at least read, this approach ignores one fundamental point. At the level of anecdote, it does not matter whether stories are true or not. They could be fact, fiction or fable – whatever they are, the stories can still be enjoyed and the moral message can still be discerned. The big problem is, however, that it *does* matter whether the stories are true or not, because these smaller stories are part of the big story of the book of Samuel, which in turn has a crucial place within the Bible's overall story of redemption. If we doubt whether men did the things attributed to them here, how can we be sure that God did what is attributed to him in these pages? The human and the divine acts stand or fall together.

2. Existential

(I) GUIDANCE

I am tempted to call reading the stories of the Bible for guidance 'the horoscope method', because some people read the Bible each day hoping that something might leap out and fit them! There are rare occasions when people have testified to a particular verse or passage having played a significant role in their lives, but this says more about God's ability to use any means he chooses to guide us than it does about the legitimacy of the method. The method completely ignores the fact that most of the verses will mean nothing to a person's particular situation. There is a classic story about a man who was thumbing through his Bible looking for a verse and found, 'Judas went out and hanged himself.' Not satisfied, he looked for another and found, 'Go and do thou likewise!'

If we are reading the Bible for a personal message, what do we make of the verse in 1 Samuel where Samuel says to Eli, 'In your family line there will never be an old man'? It was appropriate centuries later for one of Eli's descendants, the prophet Jeremiah, who started his prophetic ministry when he was 17 since he would not live to old age. But there is no application for us. Or take another verse '...and Samuel hacked Agag to pieces before the Lord.' How would this be applied?

I am ridiculing this method because I am sure that this should not be the main reason for reading these stories. The books of Samuel will reveal relatively little if this is how we read them. We need to read the text in the *context* in which it is written if we are to extract the correct meaning. If we just look for texts relevant to our own situation, we will miss an enormous amount.

(II) COMFORT

In former days 'Promise Boxes' were used by the devout in order to find encouragement to face life. Each biblical 'promise' was printed on a curled up roll of paper and one was lifted out at random with a pair of tweezers each day. Needless to say, each was also lifted out of its biblical context and therefore often separated from the conditions attached to it. For example, 'Lo, I am with you always' is placed in the context of 'Go and make disciples', and we should not claim the promise if we are not fulfilling the command. Even without such a box, we can read the Bible in much the same way, looking for a verse we can lift out for ourselves. We shall find few like this in the historical books of the Bible, like Samuel and Kings. They yield up their treasures to those who read them whole, seeking to know just what God is like, how he feels about us rather than how we feel about ourselves, or even about him.

3. Biographical

(I) INDIVIDUAL

The third method is most common among preachers. One of the great features of the Bible is the honest way it records the failures and successes of the main characters. James says in the New Testament that the Bible is like a mirror that can show us what we are like through the people we read about. We can compare ourselves with Bible characters and ask whether we would have behaved in the same way.

With this in mind, we can note how the first two kings of Israel both started well and finished badly, yet Saul was seen as the worst king and David as the best.

We read of the character of Saul, a man who was literally head and shoulders above the rest, with many personal advantages. We read how the Spirit of the Lord came upon him and he turned into a different man. But we read, too, of the fatal flaws in his character, and how his insecurities led to poor relationships and jealousy of the gifted people around him.

We can contrast Saul with David, whom the Bible calls 'a man after God's own heart'. When Samuel chooses David we read, 'The Lord does not look at the things man looks at. Man looks at the outward appearance, but the Lord looks at the heart.'

Scripture describes David as a man of the outdoors, involved in manual labour, handsome and brave. He developed his relationship with God during the lonely days and nights as a shepherd, reading the law, praying and praising God for creation as well as redemption. These years were a preparation for him to become the most important person in the land.

We can note his skills as a leader, asking God's opinion before taking any decision. Even though he was anointed as king, he refused to take the throne too soon, but waited for God's timing. He was a magnanimous man even in victory, unhappy when his enemies were killed and furious because one of Saul's surviving sons was killed, even though Saul had been his enemy. He was a very forgiving man, and a man who could honour brave people – in the book of Samuel we have a list of those whom David honoured.

David was therefore the opposite of Saul: he had a heart for God and he loved honouring other people. Saul did not have a heart for God and did not like to have anyone else who was successful anywhere near him.

There are other comparisons: Samuel and Eli shared an inability to discipline their children. Jonathan and Absalom were both sons of kings but behaved very differently. Jonathan was an unselfish son of a bad king (Saul) who was willing to surrender to David's leadership. Absalom was the selfish son of a good king (David) who wanted to seize the throne from his father.

The women in Samuel also make a lovely character study. Hannah and Abigail both reveal interesting traits. We read of Hannah's devotion to God and her excitement when she became pregnant. Abigail courageously averted a crisis by making food for David's men when her husband had refused them hospitality. She so impressed David that he married her shortly after her husband's death.

(II) SOCIAL

We can also study the relationships between individuals.

Jonathan and David's friendship is one of the most pure and godly in the pages of the Bible.

The frustrating, even threatening, interaction between Saul and David is a classic example of how difficult personal relationships can be with unreliable temperaments, who alternate between welcoming and rejecting moods, especially when there is the added complication of influence by evil spirits.

The whole saga of David and the various women in his life is full of insights into gender relationships. Nor is his ability to win the affection and devotion of the various men in his life irrelevant to contemporary society.

The people's insistent choice of their first king and their reasons for it have something to say for the influence of image on contemporary elections.

So these stories have social as well as individual implications, from all of which we can learn valuable lessons. But this still falls short of the intended message of the text.

4. Historical

(I) LEADERSHIP

A fourth way of considering Samuel is to see it as a study of the history of Israel. Israel developed from a family to a tribe, then to a nation, and finally to an empire. It is this development into an empire that is outlined in the 150 years covered by the books of Samuel.

The request for a king came from the people, jealous of the unified and visible leadership which monarchies provided in other nations around them, and fed up with the federal relationship of 12 independent tribes which pertained at that time.

Samuel warned the people that there would be heavy costs associated with any move towards a centralized government through a king. The people went ahead with their request and the course of history was set. God acceded to their request, but insisted that Israel's king should not be like kings in other nations. Israel's king must write out the law and read it daily, and provide spiritual leadership for the people (this provision in Deuteronomy shows that God had anticipated this development). Thereafter the character of the nation would be tied to the king.

(II) STRUCTURE

The move from a federal to a centralized structure for the nation was not painless. We can study the book from this standpoint, noting the struggles David faced and his skill in overcoming them. We can note how his genius as an organizer and his skill as a commander under God led the nation to reach a peak of peace and prosperity under his rule. His selection of Jerusalem as the capital city was one of a number of brilliant master strokes. The city was captured from the Jebusites and so was not regarded as the preserve of any particular tribe.

The empire grew under David, previous enemies became satellite states and all the land which had been promised was conquered for the first and last time. The Philistines no longer bothered them. But centralized government proved to be the Israelites' downfall as well, for when power is in fewer and fewer hands, the character of those people who own the hands inevitably determines what happens.

5. Critical

(I) 'LOWER' CRITICISM

Lower criticism is the study of the Bible by scholars to see if there are any errors in the text. They study and compare manuscripts in the original languages, and note any discrepancies that may have occurred through errors of transmission by the copyists. This work gives us enormous confidence that the manuscripts which translators use are very close to the original and it is believed that the New Testament is 98 per cent accurate.

The earliest of the full Old Testament manuscripts is the Masoretic text dated at AD 900. There is a complete copy of Isaiah, one of the Dead Sea Scrolls, from 100 BC which is 1,000 years older than all the other copies available. This was discovered when the Revised Standard Version was being translated, so they held back the publication until the text had been checked against this older manuscript. In fact, the text they had been working on originally was very accurate and only a few things needed to be changed.

Whilst the Old Testament text does not have the same accuracy as the New Testament, we can still be assured that there is very little which is different from the original text. Furthermore, it is worth noting that any dilemmas regarding translation are on small details and not the central truths of the faith. In Samuel, for example, there are two accounts of the death of Goliath, but only one makes David responsible. If just one letter is adjusted, the discrepancy is solved. Clearly a copyist made an error in transmission.

(II) 'HIGHER' CRITICISM

Lower criticism is a necessary and welcome discipline, but higher criticism does a great deal of damage. It came originally from Germany in the nineteenth century and filtered into many theological colleges during the twentieth century.

The basic argument of higher criticism is that even if the original text accurately conveys what the writer meant, we can still be mistaken about what we should believe. The higher critics approach the text with their own presuppositions based on what they regard as reasonable. Those who argue that science has disproved miracles omit any miraculous events from the text, while those who cannot believe in supernatural foreknowledge omit any prophecy that accurately predicts the future.

These scholars work at a purely academic and intellectual level, with little concern for or understanding of personal faith. Their approach unavoidably leaves the text of Scripture in pieces, unrecognizable from the original.

6. Theological

A theological approach to reading the books of the Bible makes every page and every sentence of value. The levels of reading we have considered so far are concerned only with the human side of Bible study, but the Bible is primarily a book about God, with only a secondary interest in God's people. This type of study asks how we can read the text in order to get to know God.

We have already seen how Samuel is a prophetic book. The history recorded is history from God's perspective, recording what God believed to be important.

Taking the theological approach, therefore, we can look at a story and ask how this event related to God. How did he feel about it? Why did the event matter so much to God that it was included for us to read as part of Holy Scripture? We start to read the book from God's point of view and draw conclusions about who he is and what he is like. Confident that God does not change, we can then apply these timeless truths to our own day and generation.

JUSTICE AND MERCY

This is the best and most exciting way to read Samuel. The book describes God's intervention in the life of Israel, for he is the real actor in these stories, not Saul, David or Samuel. God both initiates historical events and responds to them. We see how Hannah is barren, she prays, and God gives her a son. We see how David, in God's name, kills Goliath with his first stone. We see how David, with God's help, escapes the clutches of thousands of men from Saul's army. God helps some folk and hinders others. He is just in punishing evil and sometimes merciful in not punishing when punishment is deserved.

He gives Israel the land, but when they disobey him he sends oppressors. When they repent he sends deliverers. He allows the people to choose a king, but when the king fails he gives them another, one after his own heart.

We can study the stories of Samuel, learn lessons from the history and compare ourselves with Saul or David, but the real reason to read the book is to learn about the character of God.

God's activity is seen especially at the heart of the book. He makes a covenant with David, confirming his commitment to Israel which had first been expressed in the covenants with Abraham and Moses centuries before. This is the most vital moment in 1 and 2 Samuel. It arises when David asks God if he can build a house for him. He is embarrassed that he has built such a grand palace for himself and that God is living in a tent next door.

When David tells God he will build him a house, three messages come from the prophet Nathan. The first message is, 'Do it.' The second message is, 'Don't do it.' God explains that a tent is good enough for him since he never asked for a palace of stone. The third message is that David must not build the temple because he is 'a man of blood', but his son can build it.

In the covenant God tells David how he will treat his son. He will discipline him but will never cease to love him. David's house and kingdom will endure before him for ever. His throne will be established for ever; there will always be a descendant of David on the throne.

From that moment on, the descendants of David always keep careful records of their family tree, wondering if their son might be the 'son of David' mentioned in the covenant. This promise becomes the focus of national hopes for the next 3,000 years as the Jews look for the Messiah.

This covenant is a crucial theme through the rest of the Bible. A thousand years later the promise was kept when Jesus was born to a humble couple who were in the royal line. Jesus was the legal son of David through Joseph his father, but also a physical son of David through his mother Mary. He was twice over the son of David. Throughout his life he was known as the 'son of David'. The disciples recognized his right to be known as 'Messiah' (the anointed one), and this theme continues in the later writings about him and his Church. The books of Acts, Romans, 2 Timothy and Revelation all use this title to refer to Jesus. They proclaim that all authority in heaven and on earth is given to the son of David and will always be in his hands. They rejoice that God has kept that covenant with David in his son Jesus.

In the fulfilment of the covenant we see that God's promise has wider implications, as the king on David's throne rules over the Jews and Gentiles who make up his Church.

It is only when we read Samuel from a theological point of view that we can appreciate the richness of the book in terms of its message and the part it plays in the themes developed in the Bible as a whole.

Conclusion

Samuel is a history book with a difference. It is prophetic history full of interesting, bizarre, romantic and cruel stories which, brought together, reveal God's ongoing purposes for his people. God wanted us to be ruled by one man – not King David I, but King David II. The books of 1 and 2 Samuel are part of Christian history. Jesus was king of the Jews in the past, he is king of the Church today, and he will be king of the world in the future, when he will reign in justice and righteousness, and the kingdom will finally be restored to Israel.

Thus the true significance of the book becomes clear as we understand how God is involved, acting behind the scenes, shaping history and assuring his people that his kingdom will grow and one day his own son, also the son of David, will be king.

PART IV

1 AND 2 KINGS

Introduction

My history teacher at school made the subject very dull. It was all about dates, battles, kings and queens and seemed to be complicated and irrelevant. My interest was revived by reading the spoof history book *1066 and All That*, which was certainly more amusing than my school history lessons, and where any historical event was summed up as either 'a good thing' or 'a bad thing' – there was nothing in between.

The book of Kings reads a little like *1066 and All That* (though without the humour). It describes the kings of Israel or Judah as either good or bad, depending on how they reigned. Unlike the school history many of us remember, however, biblical history is utterly compelling. It is not about irrelevant dates and battles, but is a record of God's people told from God's point of view. It is not for mere academic interest either: it is absolutely vital for the whole of mankind.

Context

The book of Kings focuses on the third of the four phases in the national development of Israel's leadership. As the Overview of the Old Testament explained (page 7), the first national leaders were patriarchs, from Abraham to Joseph, then came the prophets, from Moses to Samuel. Third came the kings, from Saul to Zedekiah, and finally the priests, from Joshua to Caiaphas.

The period of the kings is covered by four books in our English Bible:

1 Samuel: Samuel to Saul
2 Samuel: David
1 Kings: Solomon to Ahab
2 Kings: Ahab to Zedekiah

In the Hebrew Scriptures this leadership phase is covered by just two books, Samuel and Kings, with the break between Samuel and Kings cutting King Ahab's reign in two and separating the prophet Elijah's life and death. When the Old Testament was translated into Greek in 200 BC, the books became too long for one scroll. Hebrew words have only consonants, so the addition of vowels in the Greek made the books twice the length. Thus the breaks into 1 and 2 Samuel and 1 and 2 Kings were determined more by translation than by design.

Kingdoms

In Hebrew the book is called the 'Kingdoms' of Israel, not 'Kings'. The word 'kingdom' has a different meaning in Hebrew. In English it refers to a land over which a sovereign rules. Thus England is part of the United Kingdom under the reign of the Queen. In Hebrew, however, the word 'kingdom' refers to the reign of a monarch, so is defined in terms of authority not area, rule rather than realm.

Furthermore, the concept of a 'reign' in the Bible is very different from in the United Kingdom, where, under a constitutional monarchy, the Queen reigns but does not rule, the power residing in the elected government. The big advantage is that the armed forces and courts of law are not under the government directly, but are responsible to the Queen. The monarchy is valued not so much for the power it wields as for the power it keeps from others.

The kings of Israel, by contrast, had absolute power. They made the rules and commanded the armed forces. There was no parliament, no voting and no opposition parties. The king ruled by decree and not by debate. His influence over his subjects was total, and therefore his character and conduct shaped society during his rule. He stood as a representative of the nation before God, but also as a representative of God before the nation.

This meant a major change in the way the nation was evaluated. During the time described in Joshua, Judges and Ruth, there was federal government and the people were judged according to their actions. In Samuel and Kings, however, the king's character and conduct decided the fate of the nation.

Selected history

Although the book is about the kings of Israel, it is not even-handed in its allocation of space to each king. For example, Omri was a king in the north whom we know from other historical sources to have had an outstanding reign, creating an extraordinary economic turnaround for the nation. Yet the book of Kings dismisses him in eight verses, because he was deficient in the one area that mattered: he did evil in the sight of the Lord. Similarly, Jereboam II had a mini golden age in the north, yet he is given just seven verses for the same reason. On the other hand, Hezekiah, who was largely a good king, is given three chapters, a single prayer of Solomon covers 38 verses, and the stories of Elijah and Elisha, who were not kings at all, take up a third of the two books of Kings.

This apparently uneven treatment occurs because the writer is not driven by a conventional historical approach. We noted in our study of Joshua that any historian has to select what is important, make connections between the events or people he has selected, and then give an explanation as to why the events led on from each other. The writer of Kings is not interested in focusing on political, economic or military history, though he may mention all these in passing. Rather, he is concerned with two aspects of each king's rule or kingdom:

1 Its **spiritual** qualities – worship, either of the God of Israel or idols
2 Its **moral** qualities – justice and morality, or their opposites

Prophetic history

Kings is the last of a collection of books known as the 'former prophets' in the Hebrew Bible and follows Joshua, Judges and Samuel. This is history from God's viewpoint. Individuals and events are mentioned because God regards them as important and necessary for future generations. A man may be a brilliant politician or economist, but God is primarily interested in his belief and behaviour.

We could rightly term these books 'holy history', for they are a record with an abiding message and a story with an eternal moral. They offer us not just a lesson *from* history, but the lesson *of* history. Those who do not learn it are condemned to repeat it.

Universal truth

There are patterns in the history of Israel which can be universally applied. Take, for example, the length of the reign of each king mentioned in the book. A good king reigned on average for 33 years and a bad king on average for 11 years. From this we can derive the general principle that good rulers last longer than bad ones, since God is in ultimate control of history and can keep good kings on the throne.

There are exceptions – not every good king had a long reign and not every bad king had a short one – but the principle is generally true and can, indeed, still be seen in the length of time modern leaders rule.

The rise and fall of the nation

Kings covers some pivotal events in the history of God's people which we need to note if we are to grasp the message of the book and understand the books which follow. The book of 2 Samuel and the early part of 1 Kings describe the powerful position of Israel on the world stage, but most of the book of Kings is concerned with the nation's downfall. Under David and Solomon the nation was eventually united, and the empire stretched from Egypt to the Euphrates. At last the Israelites inhabited all the land promised to Abraham 1,000 years before, and controlled more besides. But from Solomon's time onwards they headed downhill, through civil war and a divided kingdom to exile in a foreign land.

The national split meant that the name Israel no longer referred to the whole nation, but only to the 10 tribes of the north. The southern tribes of Judah and Benjamin were known by the name of the larger one, Judah. This distinction continues through the rest of the Old Testament.

The southern tribes of Judah and Benjamin became known as 'Jews', derived from the tribal name Judah. Before this point the people were known collectively as 'Hebrews' or 'Israelites'. This is an important distinction to bear in mind. In the New Testament John's Gospel distinguishes between the Jews in the south and the Galileans in the north. It was the Jews in the south who were largely responsible for the crucifixion of Jesus, not all the people of Israel *per se*.

A TALE OF TWO NATIONS

Kings covers the histories of these two 'nations'. The spiritual and moral standards of the 10 tribes in the north steadily deteriorated, until Assyria sent them into exile. In the south the progression downwards is less marked. There were good kings such as Hezekiah and Josiah, but eventually they went the same way as the north and were taken away to Babylon. Their forefather Abraham had been called out of Ur – now they finished up where Abraham had begun, though this time as displaced persons.

It is a salutary lesson about how easy it is to lose what has been gained. Often the duration of the demise is much less than the time it took to reach the pinnacle.

The kingdom of Israel

The kingdom of Israel went through three stages, summarized in the table below.

1. **United kingdom**

Saul	40 years
David	40 years
Solomon	40 years

2. **Divided kingdom**

10 tribes in the north – 'Israel'
2 tribes in the south – 'Judah'

War	80 years	Elijah
Peace	80 years	Elisha
War	50 years	Israel to Assyria, 721 BC

3. Single kingdom

140 years   Judah to Babylon, 587 BC

UNITY

The first stage was the 'United Kingdom', when three kings reigned in turn over the whole of Israel. The first king was Saul, who was largely bad; the second was David, who was mainly good; and the third was Solomon, who was both good and bad.

Each reign lasted exactly 40 years. The number 40 is often indicative of the length of time God tests people. Jesus was tempted for 40 days in the wilderness; the children of Israel were in the wilderness for 40 years. It is a trial period in God's sight, and all three kings failed the test. They started well, but finished badly. David received credit for being 'a man after God's own heart', but even he had a disappointing end.

The book of 1 Samuel covers Saul's 40 years, 2 Samuel covers David's 40 years and the first 11 chapters of 1 Kings cover Solomon's 40 years.

WAR

As soon as Solomon died, the north and the south became locked in a civil war that wrecked the 'United Kingdom'. The seeds of unrest had been sown when Solomon had taxed the nation heavily and confined the benefits to the south, causing the north to grow discontented. Solomon's death was the catalyst for this unrest to boil over into armed conflict.

The two southern tribes kept the capital Jerusalem and the royal line of David. The 10 tribes in the north lost both and set up their own centres of worship, at Bethel and Dan, complete with two golden calves as the focus of their worship. Since the royal line was in the south, they also elected their own king, Jeroboam.

Succession in the north proved to be rarely smooth. There were assassinations, coups d'état, takeovers. The kings were often self-elected.

For 80 years after the split, there was war between the north and the south amid increasing animosity, culminating with the tribes in the north making a treaty with Syria and Damascus to try to wipe out the two tribes in the south. Isaiah gives the details in his prophecy.

PEACE

The 80 years of war between the north and the south were followed by 80 years of peace, during which God sent two prophets who play a huge part in the book of Kings. Elijah's ministry is recorded in 1 Kings and the first two chapters of 2 Kings, and Elisha, who followed him, is a key figure in the early part of 2 Kings.

The respite did not halt the decline, however, and in 721 BC the Assyrians defeated the northern tribes of Israel and deported them from their land. They became the '10 lost tribes', never to return to the land as a nation.

After the exile of the northern kingdom of Israel, the book focuses exclusively on Judah and Benjamin in the south. It was a very small kingdom, with Jerusalem as its capital and a small amount of land surrounding it, but their kings were descended from the royal line and they knew about God's promise to David that there would always be one of his descendants on the throne.

When the northern tribes were deported, God sent prophetic warnings from Isaiah and Micah that the same would happen to the south, but this had little or no effect. The last event recorded in the book of Kings is that Judah was led into exile by the Babylonians just 140 years later.

Purpose

We come now to focus on the basic questions that should inform our reading of any book of the Bible: Who wrote the book? How did they write it? When did they write it? Why did they write it?

Who wrote Kings?

The writer of the book cannot be known with any certainty. Most Jews think it was Jeremiah and there are a number of reasons why the case for this is strong.

1 Parts of Kings are identical to Jeremiah's prophecy – even the wording is exactly the same.
2 Jeremiah is not mentioned in the book, despite being a contemporary of Josiah and at the heart of many of the events described. It would seem impossible for anyone to cover this period without mentioning Jeremiah, but if Jeremiah is the author it would be in keeping with other writers of the Bible for him to be self-effacing.
3 We know that prophets often wrote about kings. Isaiah wrote about Uzziah and Hezekiah, and God specifically instructed Jeremiah in his prophecy to write about Israel.
4 Furthermore, there was a time in Jeremiah's ministry when recalling the history of the nation would have been especially pertinent. His prophecy tells of the time when the people of God rejected his impassioned reminders that they should be obedient to the covenant and he had to pronounce curses on the nation. This would have been the appropriate juncture to write the book of Kings.

The one problem with this hypothesis is that Jeremiah was taken to Egypt in 586 BC, and he died there, yet the last part of

2 Kings exhibits remarkable knowledge of events in Babylon. It is difficult to see how these details could square with him writing the whole book. Perhaps the best solution is that Jeremiah wrote parts of Kings, with someone else finishing it. This might explain his own absence from the narrative.

Some suggest Ezekiel as another candidate. He was known to depend on Jeremiah and has a similar style. However, the date of his last prophecy is 571 BC, which argues against him being the writer. Jeremiah is the strongest candidate, but without further proof, we must leave the question open.

How was Kings written?

The book of Kings includes references to the fact that further information can be found in other sources: the Acts of Solomon, the books of the Chronicles of the King of Israel (mentioned 17 times) and the books of the Chronicles of the King of Judah (mentioned 15 times). These books are not the books of Chronicles included in the Bible. The writer is using national records woven together to communicate a lesson about history.

Parts of Isaiah are identical in wording to Kings, suggesting that either they used a common source or one borrowed from the other at certain points.

The writer covers events in the kingdoms of Judah and Israel simultaneously. It can be confusing to read about the king of Judah, followed immediately by a section on the king of Israel, but the order is deliberate. The writer wants us to understand how each kingdom was progressing in relation to its counterpart. This is vital for the narrative during the times when the two kingdoms were at war, or when intermarriage led to a time of peace.

The writer therefore used the same sort of historical methods employed today, taking material from other sources, gathering information from libraries, and so on. The difference is that his selection was divinely inspired, so that what we have in Kings is not simply history, but the Word of God.

When was Kings written?

A vital clue to the book's date is given by phrases suggesting the temple in Jerusalem was still standing, 'and still is to this day'. This suggests a date prior to the exile to Babylon in 586 BC, which was when the temple was destroyed.

However, another part of the book suggests a later date of writing. The Babylonians killed Zedekiah, the last king of Judah, having tied him up in chains and made him watch the execution of his sons before removing his eyes. The previous king, Jehoiachin, had given in to the Babylonians and was kept as a prisoner. The last thing we read in the book of Kings is that Nebuchadnezzar, King of Babylon, released Jehoiachin from prison and invited him to dine at his table. This suggests that the book was completed half way through the exile, especially as there is no mention of the people's return. It also means that someone from the royal line of David had his meals at the king's table in Babylon, and so Nebuchadnezzar unwittingly helped to keep the royal line secure.

Taking these two details together, therefore, it seems that the book was mostly written before the fall of Jerusalem, but was actually completed during the exile.

Why was Kings written?

The motivation of the writer follows naturally from the answer to the question of when the book was written.

Here is a nation that has lost its land and its capital, and has been taken away to another land. A whole generation will never see home again. They are slaves once more, their temple lies in ruins, so inevitably they have questions about their relationship with God. Where is he? Why has he allowed all this to happen? What about his promises?

The book of Kings provides the answers to these questions. It explains that the fault for the exile lies squarely with the people. God kept his promises: he promised that if the people misbehaved they would lose the land, but in spite of repeated warnings they did not listen. The history of Kings is thus a profound lesson to these people in exile.

Yet even in this dark book there is hope, because God promises never to break his part of the covenant. God says that although the people may break the covenant, he never will. He promises to bring his children back from exile. The punishment will be for a limited time only.

In fact, the people remained in the land of Babylon for 70 years. The number was not arbitrary. God had told them to let the land rest every seventh year, but they had ignored this law for 500 years, from the time of Solomon onwards. During that time, therefore, the land had missed 70 years of rest, so in one sense the 70-year exile provided the land with a chance to catch up on its holidays!

The book of Kings is saying that the exile was a disastrous time, but it was not hopeless. God had promised to keep the royal line of David going and he would do so.

Content

Solomon

As we look at the book in more detail we begin with the king who dominates the early chapters. Solomon's name means 'peace', which was appropriate since his reign benefited from the peace David had secured when building the empire. He was a good man who began well.

At the start of his reign God appeared to him in a dream and offered to give him anything he asked for. Solomon, knowing that he lacked experience, asked for wisdom. God promised Solomon not just wisdom, but many things he did not ask for besides: wealth, fame and power.

Solomon's gift of wisdom was demonstrated in the famous story of the two prostitutes who argued about a baby. Both had babies, but during the night one of the babies died, so its mother stole the other's baby and placed the dead one in its place. Solomon had to adjudicate on this most awkward situation. To whom did the live baby belong? Solomon asked for wisdom from God, and then told the women to cut the baby in half and keep half each. As soon as Solomon said this, the real mother pleaded that the baby be allowed to live and be given to the other woman. Solomon thus knew who was the true mother.

Perhaps Solomon's most memorable act was his building of the temple with the materials and the plans provided by his father David. God had promised David that he would allow his son to build the first permanent place for centralized worship, predicted in the book of Deuteronomy centuries before. It was a magnificent temple, and took seven years to build (it took 12 years to build Solomon's own palace, however).

We read that although the temple was built out of cut stone, the sound of hammer and chisel was never heard. This was a mystery for many years until someone discovered a gigantic cave the size of a large theatre at Mount Moriah near Calvary outside Jerusalem. The floor is covered with millions of little chips where the rock has been cut. The rock is so soft that it can be cut with a penknife, but when it is brought out into the open air it oxidizes and goes quite hard. All the stone for the temple came from this cave, where they cut the blocks to the exact shape needed to fit into the temple above ground.

Solomon was also responsible for the dedication of the temple. His dedicatory prayer, based on Leviticus 26 and Deuteronomy 28, is recorded at length in Kings. It mentions God's promise to bring his people back from exile if they turned back to him, a promise that became especially significant for those in Babylon when the book came out.

His reign brought great prosperity to the people of Israel. The empire stretched from Egypt to the Euphrates and included all the territory which had been promised to them. Solomon's fame spread far and wide, even reaching the Queen of Sheba, who paid him a visit and was impressed by the splendour of his palace.

The time of peace meant opportunity for leisure and learning. Solomon collected 3,000 proverbs and wrote 1,005 songs. God chose to publish just six of these songs in the Bible. My theory is that Solomon wrote a song for each of his 700 wives and 300 concubines, but God picked only the one which appears in the Song of Solomon. Incidentally, it is at this point that we really must question whether Solomon's wisdom is demonstrated in taking so many wives. That meant 700 mothers-in-law! Like so many people, he had wisdom for everybody else, but not much for himself.

The Song of Solomon is written by a young man, so much in love that God is not mentioned directly. The book of Proverbs is mostly Solomon's work, written when he was middle-aged. Ecclesiastes was written at the end of his life, and there he shares the philosophy of an old man with the young. In this book we see Solomon's whole life, with time for philosophy, music, agriculture and architecture. Although he developed many interests, none of them satisfied him and Ecclesiastes is one of the saddest books in the Bible.

BAD

Solomon's main weakness has already been hinted at – he had too many wives. This was not just for sensual pleasure, but also revealed a lust for power. Many of the marriages were politically motivated, for example his marriage to the daughter of Pharaoh. As an Egyptian she could not live in the holy city of Jerusalem, so Solomon built her a palace just north of the temple, outside the city wall. Recent excavations there have uncovered the only Egyptian artefacts in the whole of Israel.

We are therefore presented with an interesting juxtaposition: on the one hand there is the magnificent temple, built to aid Israel's worship of the one true God; on the other there is King Solomon with many foreign wives, who all brought their own gods with them and dragged people away from the worship of the God of Israel. Solomon was not the only king to marry foreign women, but no other king could match him in terms of numbers.

The building of the temple also exacted a huge cost. Solomon used forced labour and heavy taxation which enraged the northern tribes, who were resentful at having to finance a southern building, so far from their own territories. In spite of the success of the temple, therefore, Solomon was laying the foundations for national catastrophe.

Solomon was a king with a divided heart who left a divided kingdom. Soon the empire would break up. Even in Solomon's time, Hadad the Edomite rebelled, and more would follow.

Divided kingdom

The reigns of the kings of Judah and Israel are recorded differently.

NORTH	SOUTH
Date of accession	Date of accession
Length of reign	Age at accession
Formally condemned	Length of reign
Name of father	Name of mother
	Summary of character
Reference to sources	Reference to sources
Death	Death and burial
Son or usurper	Son as successor

The kings of the north are all compared to the first northern king, Jeroboam, who was a bad king. So we read repeatedly of subsequent kings: '…and he did what was evil in the sight of the Lord, just like Jeroboam.'

In the account of the kings of Judah in the south, the writer uses different records and varies the order and the details. He starts with the date when they began to reign, but follows with the king's age – Josiah was just eight, for example. The length of the reign is given next, but then comes the name of the mother, not the father, for reasons which are not clear. (Today a person qualifies as a Jew if their mother is a Jew, but in the Bible it was the father who determined nationality.) Then comes the judgement as to whether they were good or evil. Whilst every king in the north was evil, the south had a mixture of good and evil, with David as the benchmark.

The kings

The north had 20 kings and the south had the same number, but the south survived for 140 years longer than the north because, as we noted earlier, good kings reign longer. Some of the bad kings survived only a couple of months before being killed.

As mentioned above, the northern kings were all bad, although some were not as bad as the others.

NORTH 'ISRAEL' (10)		SOUTH 'JUDAH' (2)	
Prophets	Kings	Kings	Prophets
AHIJAH	**Jereboam**	**Reheboam**	SHEMAIAH
	Nadab	Abijam	
JEHU	**Ba'asha**	*Asa*	
	Elah		
	Zimri		
	Omri		
<u>ELIJAH</u>	**Ahab**	*Jehoshophat*	OBADIAH
MICAIAH	**Ahaziah**	Jehoram	
	Jehoram	**Ahaziah**	
<u>ELISHA</u>	Jehu	ATHALIAH	
	Jehoahaz	*Joash*	JOEL
	Jehoash	*Amaziah*	
JONAH	**Jereboam II**	*Uzziah*	
AMOS	**Zechariah**		
	Shallum	*Jotham*	
	Pekah		ISAIAH
HOSEA	**Manahem**		MICAH
	Pekahiah	*Ahaz*	
	Hoshea	*Hezekiah*	
		Manasseh	
	721 BC		
		Amon	NAHUM
		Josiah	JEREMIAH
Very good		**Jehoahaz**	ZEPHANIAH
Good		**Jehoachim**	HABBAKUK
Bad		**Jehoachin**	DANIEL
Very Bad		**Zedekiah**	
QUEEN		587 BC	EZEKIEL

The south had six good and two very good kings (Hezekiah and Josiah), but also had one who was the worst of all. This is the exception to the rule about bad kings and short reigns, for Manasseh reigned for 55 years.

The south had just one dynasty, whereas the north had nine, with the succession changing hands due to assassination six times.

There was one queen. God had told David there would always be a *man* on the throne – women were not allowed to rule as monarchs. Athaliah had other ideas. She was Jezebel's daughter and married the king of Judah in the south. She wanted to be the first queen of Israel, so she systematically killed all the children of David's royal line, so that the way would be open for her to become queen. However, an aunt took the youngest boy, Joash, and hid him ready to take the throne when Athaliah died, so the royal line was spared.

The two very good kings of Judah were Hezekiah and Josiah. Hezekiah was contemporary with Isaiah and his story is included in Isaiah's prophecy. Hezekiah was a good king in many ways. It was he who ordered the digging of the tunnel to bring water into Jerusalem and make it safe against enemies. His big mistake occurred when he was taken ill and welcomed to his palace men from the (then) small and unknown city of Babylon. They brought a 'get well card' and Hezekiah was flattered that someone so far away knew and cared about his illness. He showed the men round the palace and the temple. It was Isaiah who pointed out the error. He told Hezekiah that the Babylonians would take away everything he showed them. Some years later they did just that.

The other good king came to the throne of Judah at just eight years of age. Josiah was born in the same year as Jeremiah the prophet. While they were cleaning the temple his men found the scroll of Deuteronomy, which had not been read for many years. When King Josiah read the curses God had promised if his people strayed from his laws, he was alarmed and began at once to put things right. He ordered a national reformation, destroying all the high places and calling a halt to the idolatry which had infected the land, in the hope that this would bring renewal. But people's hearts remained far from God. It is not possible to make people good by passing good laws.

Josiah also made a big mistake: he went to war with Egypt when he did not need to and he was killed at Megiddo. When he died the nation reverted to the evil practices he had stamped out.

Hezekiah was followed by Manasseh, a very bad king who took evil to new depths. He worshipped the god Molech, and this included sacrificing his baby sons in the valley of Hinnon, or 'Gehenna'. He also executed Isaiah the prophet for his preaching, ordering to him to be bound and put inside a hollow tree trunk, after which two carpenters with a big saw cut the tree in half.

One of the worst kings was Ahab, who married a Phoenician princess from Tia. Her name in Phoenician meant 'primrose', but the same name in Hebrew, Jezebel, meant 'garbage', and this was how she was known. It was clear that she used Ahab to achieve her own evil ends and that he needed little persuading. It was her scheming, for example, which arranged the death of a neighbour, Naboth, so that Ahab could take possession of his vineyard.

Elijah

It was this event which marked the start of the prophet Elijah's ministry. He was a Tishbite from Gilead, in the Trans-Jordan region, and was regarded as one of the finest of Israel's prophets. Although there is no book written in his name, Kings covers more of his life than most of the kings themselves.

He is best known for his confrontation with the prophets

of Baal on Mount Carmel. Mount Carmel is 12 miles long and juts out into the ocean in the north of Israel. At the eastern (inland) end there is a large depression just below the summit where 30,000 people could gather. This must be the place where Elijah challenged the prophets of Baal, whom Jezebel had introduced to the palace. There is a spring there that never runs dry, even in a drought. The text tells us that Elijah doused the sacrifice with water, even though there had been no rain for three and a half years.

The story is well known. Elijah built an altar and challenged the prophets of Baal to build their own altar alongside his and call on their gods for fire to burn up the sacrifice.

It was a very clever challenge. We now know that the altars of Baal had a tunnel underneath where a priest would be concealed to set fire to the wood when the people cried out to the god. Elijah cunningly asked them to build their altar in the open and promised to build his altar in exactly the same way, only he would also add water to make the challenge greater. His boldness led him to mock the priests in such a way that if his experiment had failed he would surely have been killed. He encouraged them to shout louder, suggested that their god was on holiday or relieving himself. It was a key moment in the history of the northern tribes. God sent the fire, Elijah's sacrifice was burned up and Israel knew who was truly powerful. The prophets of Baal were routed.

This amazing story has an unlikely sequel. When Jezebel heard about Elijah's victory and the death of her prophets, she threatened Elijah. Despite his victory over the 400 prophets of Baal, Elijah ran for his life to Horeb. The prophet was emotionally and spiritually exhausted, so God graciously sent an angel to cook him a meal, and later assured him of his presence and provision for the future of Israel. God had already set aside a colleague for Elijah to continue the work.

Elisha

Elisha, the ploughman, succeeded Elijah in the prophetic role. He asked Elijah for a 'double portion' of his spirit – a phrase that is frequently misunderstood. It does not mean that he wanted to be twice the prophet Elijah had been. It was actually a phrase taken from the inheritance customs. If a man had four sons, his estate was divided into five when he died and the double portion went to the eldest son, who became the heir of the family business, with the extra money to help with the responsibility. In asking for a double portion of Elijah's spirit, Elisha was asking to be his heir and successor to be allowed to 'take over the business'.

Elijah told Elisha that if he saw him leave the earth, he could be his heir. Elijah was one of the few people in the Bible who never died (Enoch was another). The text tells us that he rode in a chariot into heaven, and Elisha saw him depart. Elijah's robe fell on the ground, Elisha picked it up and walked to the River Jordan. Elisha's ministry was given an excellent start, with God parting the river for him, assuring Elisha that he was with him just as he had been with Elijah.

The work of Elijah and Elisha

The two prophets were very different. Elijah was the fighter, the preacher, the man who challenged the people. Elisha's ministry was more pastoral in nature. On one occasion he raised to life a widow's son, in the village of Shunem, just half a mile from the village of Nain where Jesus would do the same thing. Elisha also fed 4,000 people with a few barley loaves. Elijah's ministry seems similar to that of John the Baptist and Elisha's to the ministry of Jesus.

Elijah and Elisha were two of a number of prophets whom God sent to the northern tribes: Jonah was a prophet to Judah before he went to Nineveh, and he appears in the book of

Kings. Amos and finally Hosea were also sent. The prophecy of Hosea contains some of the deepest emotion of all the prophets, as he enacts within his own life the heart of love God has for his people.

The amount of space given to Elijah and Elisha in Kings reminds us that God gave the people frequent warnings about what would happen if they did not behave according to his law.

God's warnings

WORDS

Throughout the spiritual demise of the nation, the priests should have been reminding the people of their responsibilities. But they were too close to the establishment to provide an objective voice, so God sent prophets instead.

There were six prophets sent to the north: Ahijah, Jehu, Elijah, Elisha, Amos and Hosea. There were also a number who ministered to the south, before and during the exile: Shemaiah, Obadiah, Joel, Jonah, Isaiah, Micah, Nahum, Jeremiah, Zephaniah, Habakkuk, Daniel and Ezekiel.

It is important to note that God always gave his people a warning of his punishment if they continued in sin. The whole principle of the Bible is that God judges people for doing what they *know* is wrong. People who have not heard about Jesus will not be sent to hell because they have not heard about Jesus, but because they have done wrong against their own conscience.

Israel and Judah ignored the messages they received, preferring the false prophets who told them that all was well and gave them false reasons for the disasters that had befallen them. The true prophets were nonetheless prepared to tell the truth and pay the price of ridicule, beatings, punishment and sometimes death.

DEEDS

The warnings God sent were not just verbal, they were also visual. The people should have seen that God's blessings were being taken away from them. Note how the warnings increased in their severity:

1 They lost territory when Hadad led Edom out of the 'commonwealth'.
2 They lost independence when the Trans-Jordan tribes came under the control of Syria and one tribe, Naphtali, was lost totally to Assyria.
3 Judah saw the other nine tribes deported to Assyria.
4 Eventually they too faced deportation to Babylon, in three stages.

Apart from the spoken prophetic messages, therefore, there were a number of warning signs from events which were clearly heading for disaster, but the people ignored these too and did not change their ways.

Why read Kings?

Christians can be sure that all parts of the Old Testament are also intended for them. We are told in 1 Corinthians that the events in the Old Testament 'occurred as examples to us from setting our hearts on evil things as they did'. In 2 Timothy we read that 'all Scripture is God-breathed and useful for teaching, rebuking, correcting and training in righteousness'.

Individual application

THE PRESENT

We may not *be* kings, but we too are examples to others, at work, in the family, in the community. Like kings, we need to set the spiritual tone for the groups we are involved with, especially if we have a leadership role.

We can be tempted to have liaisons with people who have 'foreign' gods. We must beware of the dangers of marrying outside God's family.

Kings gives us the negative example of Queen Athalia, who sought to take up leadership against the will of God. All Christians can be tempted to seek leadership for the wrong reasons, or which is inappropriate for them personally.

Josiah's reign reminds us that we must be regular readers of the Bible. We can be negligent or ignorant of its truth and face similar consequences.

The book also provides key lessons for Christian leaders, for the king had a pastoral role to exercise for his people, a role he often abused.

THE FUTURE

We will *become* kings: we too are part of the royal family, preparing to reign with Christ. We can look forward to a bright future. Even if our lives have little opportunity for leadership now, there will come a day when it will be different.

Corporate application

THE CHURCH

Just as Israel put idols on the high places in the land, Britain has a tradition of pagan shrines being situated on the hills. Christian churches now stand on many of these sites, but the danger of compromise with paganism remains. Syncretism, the uniting of one religion with another, is still around and still popular.

When Elijah challenged the people of Israel, he asked them how long they would waver *between* two opinions. The same question could be asked of the Church today, for in Britain and elsewhere there are professing Christians who see nothing wrong in mixing their faith with pagan religion and contemporary materialistic and new age philosophies. Prince Charles says he prefers to be called Defender of Faith, not Defender of *the* Faith. We are into an era when it has become fashionable to say that all religions lead to God.

Furthermore, the Church has blessed pagan festivals, often unknowingly. Christmas is the most obvious example: it was originally a totally pagan midwinter festival celebrating the 'rebirth' of the sun. The people burned yew logs, sang carols, and ate and drank too much. When the first missionary, Augustine, came to England he sent word back to Rome saying that he was unable to get the people away from this pagan festival. Pope Gregory said that the best policy would be to turn it into a Christian festival, and that is what has happened, with questionable results. Today the Church universally celebrates this pagan festival, despite the fact that it is nowhere commanded or even encouraged in the Bible.

The book of Kings also demonstrates the principle that division leads to decline. Many church fellowships can testify to this sad truth. The nation reached its height in the unity it enjoyed under David and Solomon, and then lost everything in half the time it had taken to achieve it, once that unity had been destroyed. We must be vigilant if the same thing is not to happen to us in the Church.

THE WORLD

The book has a powerful message to offer about God's sovereignty in human history. Israel is the specific focus of his dealings as he intervenes in the lives of the kings, dispensing blessing and punishment, open to their cries for help. We see how, on the whole, good kings last longer than bad ones. In the same way, God rules over *all* nations. He chooses leaders and rulers and decides how much time and space each has. He can act in justice, giving the people the ruler they deserve, or in mercy, giving them the ruler they need. He still has the casting vote even in democratic elections.

His ability to overrule in no way reduces human responsibility. He can use even those who have no knowledge of him – a bad ruler like Nebuchadnezzar to take his people into Babylonian exile and a good ruler like the Persian Cyrus to restore them to their own land again.

News agencies only see the human side of history. Prophets discern the divine activity over and above this. That is why the Bible in general and the books of 1 and 2 Kings in particular are so different from other historical records. They give us the *whole* story, telling the whole truth about what happened in the events of Israel's saga.

CHRIST

Above all, we need to read Kings because of what it tells us about Jesus. A number of individuals who feature in Kings remind us of Jesus.

- **Solomon**: Matthew tells us in his Gospel that Jesus is greater than Solomon. Paul writes that Christ is our wisdom. John's Gospel tells us that Jesus likened his body to the temple. When Jesus died the temple curtain was split from top to bottom.
- **Jonah**: The prophet is mentioned in Kings. Just as Jonah was in the belly of the fish for three days and three nights, so Jesus would be raised after three days and three nights in the heart of the earth – in both cases a resurrection from the dead.
- **Elijah**: Jesus met and talked with him on the Mount of Transfiguration. Elijah was likened to Jesus' cousin John the Baptist, who had the same food and dress.

■ **Elisha**: Jesus indirectly linked himself to Elisha through the nature of the miracles he performed. Jesus raised a boy from the dead in the village of Nain, next to Shumen where Elisha had performed a similar miracle. He fed 5,000 people with bread and fish, mirroring Elisha's miracle in feeding the 4,000 with bread. When Jesus died, people came out of their graves, just as a dead man was revived after contact with Elisha's dead body.

There are also ways in which the life and ministry of Jesus fulfil the expectations of kingship. He is the king the Old Testament people longed for. He is in the royal line of David, and will one day restore the kingdom to Israel. He is the one who fulfils all the promises made about the descendants of David. Here is one king who will not disappoint, one even greater than David.

Conclusion

The book of Kings has a vital message for the world. God is Lord over all, and his people must learn the message of this book if they are not to mirror the decline recorded there, the disintegration of the people of Israel who ceased to listen to God and follow his laws. We can, however, be encouraged by God's power and ability to deal with his people in ways that are both just and merciful. No one can thwart his plans. His kingdom will outlast the years, and the book of Kings (or Kingdoms) gives Christians a longing for the day when Jesus will be seen by all as the final king.

Christian Books

Timeless truths in shifting times

www.christian-publishing.com

News from a Christian perspective

Exclusive author interviews

Read extracts from the latest books

Share thoughts and faith

Complete list of signing events

Full catalogue & ordering

www.christian-publishing.com